P9-CEV-677

A
Cup
of
Comfort
for Grandparents

A Cup of Comfort

of
Comfort
for Grandparents

Stories that celebrate a
very special relationship

EDITED BY
COLLEEN SELL

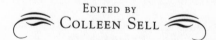

ADAMS MEDIA
Avon, Massachusetts

*In memory of my beloved grandparents: Mary and Frank Baum,
Blanche and James Sell. For my glorious grandchildren:
Brianna, John, Scott, and the sweetpea on the way.*

Copyright ©2006, F+W Publications, Inc.
All rights reserved. This book, or parts thereof, may not be
reproduced in any form without permission from the publisher;
exceptions are made for brief excerpts used in published reviews.

A Cup of Comfort is a trademark of F+W Publications, Inc.
Published by
Adams Media, an F+W Publications Company
57 Littlefield Street, Avon, MA 02322. U.S.A.
www.adamsmedia.com and *www.cupofcomfort.com*

ISBN 10: 1-59337-523-9
ISBN 13: 978-1-59337-523-2
Printed in Canada.

J I H G F E D C B A

Library of Congress Cataloging-in-Publication Data
A cup of comfort for grandparents / edited by Colleen Sell.
p. cm. -- (A cup of comfort series book)
ISBN 1-59337-523-9
1. Grandparent and child. I. Sell, Colleen. II. Series.
HQ759.9.C86 2006
306.874'5--dc22

2006014710

This publication is designed to provide accurate and authoritative information
with regard to the subject matter covered. It is sold with the understanding that
the publisher is not engaged in rendering legal, accounting, or other professional
advice. If legal advice or other expert assistance is required, the services of a
competent professional person should be sought.

 —From a *Declaration of Principles* jointly adopted by a Committee of the
American Bar Association and a Committee of Publishers and Associations

Many of the designations used by manufacturers and sellers to distinguish
their products are claimed as trademarks. Where those designations appear in
this book and Adams Media was aware of a trademark claim, the designations
have been printed with initial capital letters.

*This book is available at quantity discounts for bulk purchases.
For information, please call 1-800-872-5627.*

Acknowledgments

A bouquet of gratitude goes to each of the many who have had a hand in the making of this book—the talented authors whose stories grace these pages, the 2,000 or so authors whose stories we were unable to publish here, and the terrific team at Adams Media, particularly my *Cup of Comfort* cohorts, Kate Epstein, Kirsten Amann, Laura Daly, Carol Goff, Gene Molter, and Beth Gissinger, and *Cup of Comfort*'s grand poo-bahs, Gary Krebs and Paula Munier.

I thank Heaven above for the people who were my inspiration for this book—my beloved grandparents, whom I miss every day, and my grandchildren, whom I cherish more each day.

And thank you, dear readers, for allowing us to share these wonderful stories with you.

Contents

Introduction • Colleen Sell........................ix

When the Time Is Right • Camille Moffat 1

Grandpa in Charge • Art Montague 9

She's Back and She's Brought Something with Her •
 Denise Heins................................14

Actually, That's My Grandpa • Susan Billings Mitchell ...18

When the Going Gets Tough, Get Grandma •
 Reneé Willa Hixson.......................... 23

A Grandfather's First Letter to His Grandson •
 Mike Tolbert................................ 28

The Indomitable Miss Chelsea • Anne C. Watkins...... 34

My Granddaughters, My Life • Charles Langley........ 40

Toy Box Confidential • Darla Curry.................45

How Do I Love Thee? • Libby Simon................. 50

Raising Adam • Miriya Kilmore 56

How to Spoil a Grandchild and Alienate a Daughter-in-Law
 in One Easy Lesson • Sheila Moss 65

The Flavors of the Mix • Sydney Argenta 69

Birth of a Family • Samantha Ducloux Waltz 76

Nonna's Way • Isabel Bearman Bucher 85

What to Name a Grandmother • Glenda Baker 96

Learning to Share • William M. Barnes. 101

Jooots and Ohk • Susan J. Siersma 108

Lord, Love a Duck • Ginger Hamilton Caudill 112

The Froufrou Room • Jodi Gastaldo 121

Tender Hearts • Cathy Elliott 126

Vindication • May Mavrogenis 131

Me, a Grandmother? No Way! • Jo Ann Holbrook 136

Not for a Very Long Time • Bobbi Carducci 144

Life Cycles • Virginia Rudd 148

Grandma Will Save Me • Dennis Jamison 152

An American Babushka • SuzAnne C. Cole 157

Grumpy and Poopy Doo • William M. Barnes 163

A Valentine for a Neat Kid • Mary Brockway 170

Sounds of Love • Sally Kelly-Engeman 179

The Land of That's Okay • Valerie Kay Gwin 184

Love-a-Bye • Mahala Church 190

Tales in a Teapot • Karna J. Converse 199

Pieces of Eight • Nancy Baker. 204

Fast Track to a Teen's Heart • Dianna Graveman 210

Like Hummingbirds to Nectar • Rakel Berenbaum 216

Mama's Patootie Pie • Beverly A. Coleman 221

Legacies and Lifelines • Audrey Yanes 231

Mud Pies • Barbara W. Campbell 237

Through the Eye of a Child • Carol Ann Erhardt 245

Keeper of the Magic • Marcia E. Brown 250

Something about Daniel • Sonja Herbert. 255

Malt Balls and *Dallas* • Linda Holland Rathkopf........261

Gamma and the Car Seat • SuzAnne C. Cole.........266

Little House of Treasures • Laura L. Cooper 271

Just Call Me Grandma • Samantha Ducloux Waltz......278

The Memory Shirt • Mary Lou Cook.................282

For Immediate Delivery • Pat Fish 287

They Only Have Eyes for Pop-Pop • Margaret A. Frey....294

Giant Flogging Monster • Gaylia Roberts 301

Tell Your story in the Next *Cup of Comfort!*........... 308

Contributors....................................310

About the Editor 323

# Introduction

"*Grandchildren are the dots that connect the lines from generation to generation.*"

—Lois Wyse

I am one of *those* grandparents. You know the kind I'm talking about—the quintessential picture-toting, cookie-baking, memory-making, brag-about-'em, spoil-'em-rotten, soft-place-to-fall, crazy-about-those-little-darlings Grand of Grands. And I'm not a bit ashamed to admit it. I figure that after being the heavy for all those years raising my children, I have earned the right to shower theirs with unabashed, unconditional, uninhibited love. Nothing makes me happier.

I'm not sure how or why I became such a doting grandparent, though I suspect it has something to do with the grands in my own life. One thing I do know for sure is that it was instantaneous—love at first sight—starting from the moment I saw my first grandchild stick his thumb in his mouth, when he was still in his mommy's tummy, during an ultrasound. I whooped and laughed out loud, even as tears misted my eyes and I suppressed the urge to clobber the technician who'd poked him to make him raise his legs. I knew then that I'd protect my grandson as fiercely as I would my own children. But I also sensed it would be different, that there would be less work and worry and more play and ease. Almost seventeen years and three grandchildren later, I am happy to report that my instincts were mostly right. In fact, it's even better than I thought it would be.

Now, I know not all grandparents are as enamored with this grandy role as I am. There are many ways to be a terrific grandparent, and my jubilant, "in there" brand of granding doesn't jibe with everyone. Frankly, it sometimes drives my daughters and their husbands nuts. But they're also really glad that I'm crazy about their kids and that their kids are crazy about their "Grammie Nut."

Yep, that's me: Grammie Nut. Singer of silly songs. Weaver of goofy stories. Teller of corny jokes. Breaker of rules. Maker of yummy treats. Instigator of fun and games. It was while playing a rollicking game of Candy Land with my eldest grandson, when he was not quite four and not yet able to read, that I officially became Grammie Nut. Scott, my grandson, landed on a space and drew a card instructing him. He handed me the card and I dutifully read: "Go to Grandma's Nut House." Then, I crossed my eyes and said, "You can't go to Grammie Nut's house! You're already at Grammie Nut's house!" Amazingly, the little guy actually got my joke (did I mention he's brilliant and has a great sense of humor?) and laughed so hard he fell back on the floor, flat on his back. From that day forward, I've been Grammie Nut.

My kids had their own goofy grandparent, the one who got down on the floor and played with them and who joshed and joked with them . . . my dad, a.k.a. "Clyde" (his alter-ego, the "knucklehead" he blames whenever he breaks something, including wind). I also had mine, Grandpa Baum, whose dry wit, delivered in his gravelly voice with its strong Brooklyn accent, always makes me smile, just remembering. From those two jokesters, I learned not only how to be a fun-loving grandma but also how to be an affectionate, attentive, and accountable one. Just as my grandfather was always there to listen, advise, comfort, and help, so too has my dad always been there for my children.

For all his silly antics, my dad is also the original Dudley Do-Right—a truly good man who religiously practices the Golden Rule. It is one of the things his grandchildren love and respect most about him. It is also one of the things I most loved and respected about my dad's dad, Grandpa Sell, and something I strive to emulate for my grandchildren.

From both of my paternal grandparents, Blanche and James Sell, I learned the importance of integrity, self-sufficiency, spirituality, and family. Childhood visits to their farm are among my most cherished memories. They inspired me to provide my grandchildren with the same wealth of memories and a living example of how to live honorably and purposefully.

From my maternal grandmother, Mary Baum, I learned to be my own woman. She also inspired in me an appreciation of art, music, and literature. Her daughter, my mother, has nurtured these same qualities in my children, along with a love of nature, as I have with my grandchildren.

Being a grandparent is passing love, wisdom, and joy from generation to generation. It is, indeed, grand.

The delightful stories in *A Cup of Comfort for Grandparents* celebrate many unique facets of the grandchild-grandparent relationship. Most of the stories are written from the grandparents' perspective; some are from the parents' or the grandchild's point of view. I hope you enjoy them.

—Colleen Sell

When the Time Is Right

I t's a sad day when a person has to begin a story by defending herself. But given the subject matter I feel I have no choice. Most mothers cry when their children leave the nest. I cried every time I thought they wouldn't. As a dear old friend once explained, "The teenaged years are designed to be as awful as they are so that mothers might be willing to at least consider the potential opportunities of living in an empty nest."

I was more than willing to consider those potential opportunities. And when my children—one by one—left (fled?) the nest, I stood at the doorway, fluttered a hanky, and called out, "Take care! Don't forget to write!"

Naturally, they kept coming back. Most notably around dinnertime.

When my middle child got married and took up residence with her new husband not a ninety-second drive from my front door, her friends warned her about mothers who drop in without warning, day after day, month after month, year after year. To this, my wise daughter responded, "You don't know my mother. I'll have to make an appointment with her no less than a week and no more than thirty days before the expected visit, and she'll charge me for her time if I keep her waiting."

Let's not exaggerate, shall we? I only did that once.

In all honesty, she and I visited frequently during her early days as a new wife. I define "visited" as her showing up at the kitchen door and asking me what I was doing and if there might be a fresh pot of coffee handy.

I'm not the huggy-kissy type. I never have been. When my daughter (a teenager back then) and her date hastened off to a limo and the prom, my gentle words to her were, "If you get pregnant, I'll kill you."

Sage advice if ever there was any. I beg to report: She heeded my maternal warnings and did not become pregnant until well ensconced in her role as a wife.

Eleven weeks into the pregnancy, I got a frantic phone call from her. By this time, I lived an entire state and two hours away. It was a Friday night, and she was cramping and bleeding. Her doc had told her this was nothing to worry about. As I said, my daughter is wise, and she knew her doc was wrong.

We spent the weekend on the phone together, talking, waiting, praying. By late Sunday night it was all over. The baby had died, and a trip to the ER ended the matter. By Monday morning, my daughter and her husband stood at my front door. She looked pale. He looked sad. I said, "You need to eat. Come in."

They stayed five days.

She said to me, "I hate God for letting my baby die. I guess I'm going to Hell."

I said, "You're not the first of His children to hate Him, and you won't be the last. He's been God a long time, and He's pretty tough. He can handle it."

A few months later she called to tell me she was pregnant again. I thought, *Here we go.*

Through daily e-mail reports and pictures garnered from the Internet, I was kept apprised of my grandchild's development. Blurry black-and-whites depicted blobs vaguely resembling something that vaguely resembled a baby, beneath which descriptive notations were written. "Mom! This is what Baby Pie looks like now! See? Fingers and toes!"

Squint though I might, I never managed to find fingers and toes. The first time she sent me a picture like that, I thought it was a map of India and it was her way of telling me they were moving.

Eventually, Baby Pie had both a gender and a name. A sonogram revealed a little girl (this determined by the lack of obvious little-boy plumbing), and her parents named her Naomi.

Well, then, "Naomi" it is.

I would peer at more pictures of white blobs and whisper, "Hey, Naomi. Eventually, you and I are going to have a little talk. For now, however, I'd be content if you could manage to sprout visible fingers and toes. Your mother knows I'm lying when I say I can see them."

In time, my daughter and son-in-law asked me if I would be present when Naomi finally made her debut. It was on the tip of my tongue to remind them that I need a week's notice to drive to Virginia. I'm sensitive, you know. I need to plan things.

As it turned out, Naomi's parents were at my house when she first began her approach to the exit ramp. Again, a Friday night. Naomi's father and grandfather did what men do during these high-stress, life-altering situations. They went to sleep. My daughter and I walked the floor for hours. Okay, that's not entirely true. My daughter walked the floor for hours. I sat in a chair and lovingly encouraged her. "Come on! Knees up! You can do this!"

On Saturday, Naomi stalled and her parents returned to Virginia and their apartment to wait it out. I napped at home. All that cheering was exhausting. By Monday, Naomi seemed to have made up her mind, and off to I went to the hospital.

While I have given birth to several babies myself, I'd never actually seen a baby being born. Those surgical drapes they use during C-sections really spoil the view. The only information I had regarding the birth process at all, I got from television. Yet there I was, in a hospital room on the verge of The Real Deal.

My daughter is not only wise, she's tough—a lot tougher than I had ever given her credit for being. All day, the contractions continued. All day, Naomi opted to stay put. Into the night, I watched a fetal monitor and wondered about my granddaughter, *What in the hell are you waiting for?* I held my daughter's hand, gazed silently into her pleading hazel-green eyes, and thought, *Will you please come on, kid?*

Finally, the pushing. With my son-in-law on one side of my daughter and me on the other, we each held one of her legs while she reached around, grabbed her thighs, pulled forward, and pushed. It seemed to go on for hours, only because it actually went on for hours.

The doc arrived, measured the situation, and got to work. My granddaughter was born with a suction cup attached to her head. I found her stubbornness prophetic but decided not to mention it.

After she was born, I stepped back and got out of the way. The doctor had work to do. The pediatric nurse had work to do. The new parents were making excited introductions to their new progeny, and Miss Naomi needed a few moments to get a handle on the whole idea of oxygen passing through her lungs and the fact that life on the other side is bright, cold, and loud.

Eventually, though, this little person was properly swaddled and handed to me. I looked into her dark eyes, and she looked back. I didn't blink, and neither did she. I said, "We have a lot to talk about . . . later."

Naomi's extended family crowded into the room, and I watched her being passed from one pair of eager arms to the next. She did not cry, did not protest at all. I thought, *She is not afraid. That's something. My granddaughter is brave and inquisitive.*

Her eyes met the eyes of every person who held her, and I thought, *She is direct. No nonsense. That's something, too. My granddaughter is intelligent and not afraid to question things.*

After Naomi and her mother were released from the hospital, the entire little family came to stay with me. My job was to take care of my daughter (and feed her husband) while she took care of her daughter. Naomi and I had a few moments together, here and there, but not many.

But I kept watch. I noted everything. When I held her, I pressed her face close to mine so she could breathe on me and I could know her spirit. I had so much to tell her, but not then—later, when the time was right.

Naomi is eight months old, this very day. During those eight months, I have held her face close to mine many times. I have pressed her gently against my heart so I could feel her heart. I have met her gaze with my own and whispered, "You have come from great women, Naomi. You were born to be strong and wise and brave. I have so much to tell you."

She now bounces to music, which is only natural. Her mother is a dancer, as was one of her great-grandmothers. Her grandfather is a musician.

I hold her in my arms and rock softly from heel to heel. I can hear her breathing, feel the warmth of her breath against my neck. I remember her mother breathing warmly against my neck so many years ago.

I say to her, "Naomi, there are a million stars in the sky and they make constellations. I know their names and will teach you how to see the Big Dipper, the Great Bear, and the belt of a mighty warrior in the night sky. I will teach you the love of words and stories. I will point to deer and wild turkeys and groundhogs, perhaps even a fox if the ground is snowy enough and we are keen enough. I will teach you about all the great women who came before you and made you who you are. You will have your great-great-grandmother's wisdom and natural elegance.

You will have your great-grandmother's courage and strength. You will have the freedom of spirit that came to you from your father's mother, and from me you will have stories and histories and a sense of 'knowing' I could never explain. Your mother has it. You will, too. And from your mother you will also have kindness, warmth, stubbornness, and a powerhouse intellect.

"Be strong. Be confident. And know that the blood of your ancestors races through your veins and straight into your heart."

I sit her on my lap, and she reaches for my fingertips. I curl my fingers around hers. My eyes follow the curve of her face, my hand about her chest feels her beating heart, and I promise her, "As long as I am here, Naomi—as long as God allows—I will hold your hand, believe in you, tell you stories and remind you of your powerful truths."

She turns her head and looks at me, straight into my eyes, and I know she has heard me, because I can feel her ancient spirit mingle with my own.

My daughter stands over us, watching. She reaches for her baby and says to me, "Don't you just love her, Mom?"

I smile and wink, "She'll do."

—Camille Moffat

Grandpa in Charge

Sometimes, when K.C.'s parents are away on business, she and Grandpa—that's me!—get to spend the day together. I'm put in charge. On one such day, K.C., just two years and a bit, was definitely feeling up for her special time with "Pa," as she calls me.

Sometime during the night before or in the pre-dawn hours, K.C. had mastered the infamous "toddler crib climb." When I brought her orange juice at 6:30, she was sitting amid her pillows, bed sheets, and assorted stuffed animals on the floor outside her railed crib, looking nonchalantly at her picture books, which she had spread all around her. Her eyes shone with mischief as she watched my startled reaction.

I was horrified; she could have tumbled on her head. I ran for my toolbox and quickly converted the crib to a normal bed as K.C. watched. She clapped her hands, pleased as punch. It was almost as if she knew that the crib-climbing feat was a major toddler rite of passage. She was now a "big kid," no nonsense about it.

By 8:00, K.C. had eaten breakfast and we were bound for the playground. The day seemed to be leveling out. Sanity would prevail. Ah, what a delightfully adult sense of control I had when we started out on our adventure.

Other little people were already at the playground, including some obvious four-year-olds. I can always spot the four-year-olds. They have aggressive ways and sharp tongues. Plus, because K.C. is tiny for her age, the monster-sized four-year-olds feel obliged to try to pick her up, push her swing too high, and show her how to throw sand, eat sand, and fill her shoes with it. She already knew the many uses of sand, including filling Grandpa's pockets and taking samples home, usually secreted in her sun hat.

I hung fairly close to K.C. as she moved among the playground pieces. Some, like the swinging tires and rope ladders, still defy her. She always seems pleased when I'm there to do a rescue if she gets hung up or suddenly realizes her initial idea was maybe not so hot, even if she'd just seen another kid do it.

Frankly, I have more fun when we're alone at the playground, because I'm not so self-conscious dangling on one end of the seesaw or sitting on the bouncing, spring-driven plastic dinosaur showing K.C. how it works and where to put her feet and hands. I try to be instructive in a mature adult fashion, recognizing that imitation is an early childhood learning tool. And it works. Plus, I do have fun; I admit it. I have fun because K.C. does.

But this day at the playground was laden with significance, for K.C. had shown by her earlier actions that she was now a big kid. That meant, in her view, that she was ready for the big slide. To reach it required going up eight or so round ladder rungs spaced nearly a foot and a half apart—not easy when one's legs are only about eighteen inches long from hip to ankle. Twice she missed her footing and barked her shin. K.C. doesn't relate well to pain yet. On one hand, she finds it distracting; on the other, she knows a kiss will make it better. So I did some shin kissing, and finally she was up the ladder.

Next she had to cross a rope bridge, about ten feet of it. For safety's sake, I had no choice but to go up the ladder behind her, barking my shins, and help her navigate the treacherous bridge. One misstep, she is so wee, and she could plummet to the ground. This meant I had to walk the rope bridge, not touching her, of course, for she's hell-bent independent, but close enough to grab her. *Who would grab me?* I wondered.

In fearless fashion, K.C. danced across like a prima ballerina. I stepped cautiously, the rope bridge swayed, I hung on wherever I could. When I was halfway over, K.C., on the other side, began to rock the bridge. I bit the bullet and took two long steps. I was across, finally firmly planted on the platform that exits onto the slide, a spiral affair.

K.C. laughed. Then, like a dervish in the desert, she was gone, vanished down the slide.

My first thought was, *I'm too old for this*—meaning, trying to keep up with her. My second thought: *I'm not crossing that bridge thing again*. My third: *Where has she gone; is she all right?*

I hunkered down to get under the slide's guardrail and launched myself down the slide. What a rush! I was thin enough to fit the trough as easily as a four-year-old, but I had the weight to really move.

K.C. stood at the bottom of the slide. She was in awe, bug-eyed and gape-jawed. Grandpa had never come down a slide before. In her experience, I suspect, no really big person had ever come down a slide before. Finally, she assembled her face into a grin; she had weighed the circumstances and had reached a decision. Then she clapped her hands and shouted, "Again, Pa," and ran for the ladder.

"Pa," meanwhile, sat in a pile of sand at the bottom of the slide looking sheepishly at several obviously shocked young matrons on nearby benches. *You should be watching your charges, not me,* I thought.

After scrambling to my feet and brushing the sand from my clothes, I talked fast. I informed the ladies that I was involved in a new early education technique called "participatory parenting." That drew a few nods, snickers, and knowing looks, and luckily for me, I was not in a position to respond. My priority called, already at the top of the slide again. I headed back for the ladder, where even the four-year-olds had now gathered to share in this new participatory experience.

There were no mishaps that day at the playground. But I must confess that my mantle of leadership weighed heavily, and it was not to be taken off before a few more slides and a side trip to the chiropractor the following day.

—*Art Montague*

She's Back and She's Brought Something with Her

I got the call just four days shy of my thirty-ninth birthday. My daughter babbled about relatively unimportant gossip and tidbits for several minutes before she got around to the meat of the matter.

"Mom, can I come stay with you for a while? It's just not working out between us."

I struggled for a comforting reply while phrases such as *Never!* and *Over my dead body!* jogged through my mind.

"Sure, honey. For as long as you need us," I managed to squeak out in a sweet, motherly tone.

The following day we drove the few hours to her house to help with the move. As we pulled into her driveway, I realized with a jolt that I might have overlooked one rather tiny detail. My daughter was carrying a small package all wrapped up in blue blankets. The blanket wiggled, and a tiny head popped out. As a fairly young grandmother with a career, I had not spent a lot of time with my grandson. I eyed him with suspicion and wondered to myself why I hadn't considered this aspect of the situation. What had I been thinking? That she would put him in temporary storage?

I had a lot of questions that afternoon. I grilled my daughter on what I considered were the "issues." I hadn't changed a diaper in over twelve years. Would I be expected to do that? I liked things quiet around the house so I could work at my fledgling real estate career. Did it make a lot of noise? What did it eat? Just bottles or real food? And most important, in my opinion, did it sleep through the night? My daughter laughingly fielded all of my questions and poked a lot of fun at me for being so silly. I still had my doubts, but decided she had a point. It would be all right.

As it turned out, Baby James did not sleep through the night. I awoke around 4:00 A.M. to a loud wailing that would have a mama howler monkey beaming with pride. I tossed and turned. I got up and shut the bedroom door and returned to bed, and tossed and turned again. The howling continued. The child was starting to resemble a bad Damien movie. I struggled to stay put in my warm bed. After what seemed like hours and still no let up in the howling, I could take no more. I struggled from my warm and comfy cocoon and shuffled down the hall toward her room. The noise was ear-splitting. Halfway there, I met up with my daughter lurching down the hallway like she'd been on a three-day drunk—except that the bottle in her hand was meant for the little noisemaker.

"What's wrong with him?" I asked her in a semi-hysterical screech.

"Nothing's wrong. He's just hungry. He'll go back to sleep in a minute. It'll be all right," she responded grumpily, and staggered off to give the bottle to the howler baby.

As the weeks flew by, he did eventually start sleeping through the night. And before long he was attempting his first steps and had started eating real human food. Well, "eat" might be a bit of a stretch. I actually witnessed my husband gag as James cheerfully spit up a large chunk of chicken and smiled merrily at us all.

We've even overcome the diaper-changing challenge. I had been dreading this event and was appalled when, from all indications, a number-two diapering event was imminent during my sitter duty. Horrified, I looked to my husband for help. We huddled and devised a plan. I grabbed the diaper, and he grabbed the butt wipers. Working as a team, we managed to change the diaper in record time and dispose of the deposit with no incidents.

Recently, we celebrated his first birthday, complete with a large, blue, hairy cake that was supposed to be

Cookie Monster. After two pieces of cake, James very much resembled Papa Smurf, and he kept clapping his hands, fascinated when they stuck together with blue frosting. Papa didn't gag a single time and had a look on his face I've never seen before—one of great love and supreme indulgence. I found bits of blue frosting in the kitchen for days, but I didn't mind. We've both become silly, beaming grandparents.

As his first one-year-old bedtime rolled around, my daughter bathed the little tyke in water quickly turned blue from cake frosting. Boats and Tigger and Winnie floated merrily as he splashed water all over my bathroom. She crammed him into one-piece pajamas with feet that make his toes scrunch up funny. My daughter brings him in, smelling wonderfully of baby and lavender, to kiss Nana and Papa goodnight, a nightly ritual now, and then he is whisked off to bed for a good night's sleep.

It is blessedly quiet, and we enjoy a wonderfully calm evening of watching television and reading, and then toddle off to bed ourselves. I hear him stirring around 3:00 A.M.

Too much cake, I think to myself. And as I roll over and drift back toward sleep, I realize that everything is, indeed, all right.

—*Denise Heins*

Actually,
That's My Grandpa

I love my grandpa. He's really big and higher in the sky than I am. Actually, I wish I were up there. I want to be just like him. We measure all the time. Grandma says I'm growing.

I always go to Grandpa's house. It's the yellow one on the corner. You know, the one with pink roses that go up and over and down the front porch. Grandpa says I can pick them if I want to, but I learned about the stickers. One day I learned about the bees. I just look at the flowers now.

Grandpa lets grapes grow on his fence. He calls it a "picket" fence. Ha, ha! I think that's a funny name. When the grapes are green they make you sick. It takes them a long, long time to get purple. Then we make juice and jelly.

Last summer I climbed the big apple tree in Grandpa's backyard. Well, actually, Grandpa lifted me up to the high branches for a while. I got some apples. My brother and Grandpa got a whole bunch of apples, so we gave them to Grandma to make us an apple pie.

One time Grandpa showed me how to whittle. Actually, he whittled for me. He made an awesome whistle out of a stick. It really works. I can slip the bark up and down. It blows real noises.

Whenever it snows, Grandpa makes me a path with his rectangle shovel. (We use his triangle shovel in the garden and his rectangle shovel in the snow.) Last year we made a great big snowman. We made it wave to passing cars. Actually, I wanted it to be a policeman, so Grandpa let me use his old mailman hat. It looked like a real policeman hat. I put it on our snowman's head all by myself (when Grandpa boosted me).

My grandpa can do anything. Actually, he's the greatest. But I just learned a secret. It's a great, big secret, the best secret ever, and it's really true. It's about my grandpa. Actually, I wasn't supposed to find out. You see, I went over to Grandpa's house last night, like I always do. I just walked right in like I always do, 'cuz Grandpa says his house is my house too. Well, I walked in all right, but Grandpa wasn't in his easy chair. I called out to him, but he didn't answer me. I knew he was there. He had to be there, because all the lights were on and a fire was burning in the fireplace. Actually, he had to be there because the door was not locked.

I figured I'd better go find him, so that's what I set out to do. First, I looked in the kitchen. No one was there, not even Grandma. That was strange. She is always busy in the kitchen. I found the cookies, though. Actually, they were in the cookie jar where they always are, but I am supposed to get one every time I visit Grandma's kitchen.

Grandpa wasn't in the den. I saw the picture he is painting. It has lots of sheep in it. Sometime, Grandpa is going to teach me how to paint. Actually, he doesn't want me to touch his paint stuff yet.

I went clear out to the back porch room. I called out, "Grandpa!" He didn't answer me. Grandma didn't answer me either. I was almost ready to worry when I heard noises coming from the bedroom.

The door wasn't really open and it wasn't really closed. I just peeked into the room. There was my grandpa. He was wearing fuzzy clothes like I had never seen him wear before. They were red, all red. Not from painting red, but they were really red, all over. His boots were black and shiny, shiny, shiny.

I could not believe my eyes. My big, strong grandpa was sitting there letting Grandma paint his face. His nose was red, and she was putting girl's makeup on his cheeks. I wanted to laugh out loud. Actually, I didn't dare move or make even a sound.

Grandpa was funny when Grandma started sticking white hair onto his chin. He said it tickled him. He said he couldn't kiss her with that fluff on his face.

She teased him back. "You'll have to when I find the mistletoe," she said.

I watched Grandma brush off his shoulders. She handed him a big, black belt with a huge gold buckle.

"Put on these green mittens, and we will be ready for a picture," she said.

Something magic happened when she placed a red, pointed hat on his head. With my very own eyes I saw it. My grandpa turned into . . . *Santa Claus!*

Wow, I thought to myself, I am related to Santa Claus! Actually, that is when he spotted me.

"Where did you come from?" he asked me.

"Where did you come from?" I asked him back.

Grandpa started to laugh like a bowl full of jelly, just like the real Santa laughs. Actually, I knew it was Grandpa, but he'll probably fool everybody else.

"Well, sit on my knee, Sonny, and tell me if you have been a good boy this year."

"You know he has," said Grandma.

She pulled out her camera and started taking pictures.

"I'm glad you came," she said. "Your grandpa is on his way to be Santa's helper."

"Santa's helper?" I said.

Sounded like a good job to me. We went into the living room to take more photos by the fireplace. Grandma kept talking.

"You know, there are so many good boys and girls these days," she said, "that poor old Santa Claus can't make the rounds to talk to all of them and still have energy to make all the toys."

"I get it," I said. "That's why he wants Grandpa to help him, right?"

Grandpa let out another Santa Claus laugh. *Ho, Ho, Ho!*

"You must come to visit me at the store," he said. "You can sit on my lap like the other children."

"He'll give you a candy cane, too," Grandma piped in. "But you will have to keep the secret. Don't tell anyone. Okay?"

"I promise," I said as Grandpa gave me a huge, Santa Claus hug.

Actually, I don't blame Santa for choosing my grandpa to be his helper. I would have chosen him, too.

—*Susan Billings Mitchell*

When the Going Gets Tough, Get Grandma

My dad died when he was fifty-two. He left a wife, five practically grown children, and a fourteen-year-old boy. My mother had to work full-time. We all had to work full-time—except for my little brother. He got the summer off. Losing his father had taken its toll, and he just needed to be at home. But he was not alone. Grandma was there. She cooked and cleaned and did crossword puzzles. She studied her Bible and worked in the small patch of yard that surrounded our green, single-wide trailer.

What was a young teenage boy grieving for his father supposed to do with a seventy-five-year-old grandmother all summer? Certainly, attacking crossword puzzles for weeks on end was no rainbow in a storm. Grandma and Grandson, together in a small trailer. What was there to do?

More than one could ever imagine.

During those three tender months, Grandma and Grandson destroyed the theory of the generation gap. The lament that people sixty years apart could not relate was ignored. Instead of reaching for a frying pan or a good book, Grandma washed out a tin can and told her grandson to go dig some worms to fill it with. Then Grandma and Grandson walked to a murky lake less than a mile from the trailer park. That summer they fished the tiny bays, the creek inlets, and the steep banks of the lake. I didn't hear the conversations. I wasn't there to feel the hot sun. I have no memory of the succulent flavor of trout pan-fried in a light batter. I wasn't there. It was just my grandma and my little brother.

What I did witness was the transformation of my brother. The daily fishing excursions worked like magic. He gradually began to relax. His skin turned a dark brown. He talked more. Laughed more. His grandma had practically become his best friend.

For my little brother, as well as for the rest of us siblings, the next ten years were filled with school activities, sports, and part-time jobs. Still, Grandma was an active part of our daily lives. Then, suddenly, Grandma was gone. Baked her last pie. Filled in her last crossword. Fished with her last grandchild. We were left with memories of her . . . and a replacement: my mother. By then, most of us kids had married and had families of our own. Now, Mom was Grandma to twenty-two grandchildren, including my four children.

Like all extended families, mine has had good times and bad times: serious illness, moves to new neighborhoods, a husband and father working overseas for months at a time, a troubled teen. When the SOS went out, my mom, the grandma, never hesitated to come and help. Whether by train, plane, or Trailways bus, she would climb aboard and head for the crisis.

I'll never forget the time Mom debarked the large Amtrak train after a long night of traveling through the Cascade Mountains of the Pacific Northwest. Her hair was cut short and sported a soft gray-blonde rinse. She looked refreshed and "pumped" for the task at hand. We lugged her suitcases into the van and headed home, where the troubled teen who had prompted my SOS call was on restriction and no doubt sulking. I figured, if anyone could reach him, his patient and kind grandma could.

Grandma entered the house like a modern Mary Poppins. Although she was much shorter than Julie Andrews and could not sing a note, her grandchildren flocked to her side. One grandson picked her up and swung her around. Grandma gave hugs to everyone, even the recalcitrant one, and she paid no mind to the mumbled "Oh, hi" she received in response. Then, predictably, she took off her coat and picked up a broom. This was so like her mother, the grandma of our memories, the grandma who had taken my brother fishing when his world had fallen apart. Soon there would be crossword puzzles to fill, the garden to tend, and meals to cook. As Grandma swept her way through the kitchen, the music started.

"Listen to this," said my usually morose, of late, teenager, popping a CD into the player. "It's so cool. You'll love it!"

The drums thundered. The bass guitar wailed so loudly I thought I would lose some of my hearing. Fortunately, I had gone into the laundry room where it was quiet enough for me to form at least one coherent thought in the midst of the musical mayhem: Get that rebellious kid to turn off his music before he scares Grandma all the way back home. Before I could open my mouth and yell out this command, Grandma scooted to the laundry room and leaned her broom against the wall. She wasn't angry. She wasn't quivering. Her face was not even red.

"I'd better quit sweeping so I can concentrate on my grandson's music," she said as she turned to go back to the kitchen. "He's got a great new CD."

At that point, I forgot why I had even gone to the laundry room. Her next words completely floored me.

"After years of the grandkids' music, it's kinda growing on me."

I watched in stunned silence as she walked out of the laundry room. If she had started to bop and sway at that point, I couldn't have been any more surprised.

I stood inside the laundry room and listened in on the conversation in the next room. It was not easy, considering the loud, pulsating beat blasting from the kitchen, but I strained to hear every word. It was glorious. Tonic for my soul. My child eagerly talked with his grandma about his favorite band, sharing interesting details and his intimate thoughts and feelings. This child, who was struggling with the usual ups and downs of being a teenager, had been tense and angry and withdrawn. He needed a friend. And he found one in Grandma.

Fishing. Listening to rock music. It's all the same. A bridge from one generation to another. A way for a seasoned soul to touch the troubled heart of a young one. I shook my head in wonder. Grandma had done it again. Peace, pulsating and upbeat, spread from the kitchen and filled the house. Talk about the circle of life.

—*Reneé Willa Hixson*

A Grandfather's First Letter to His Grandson

My Dear, Beloved Mack:

You are late. We were told you would be here on Monday, and now it is Thursday. What are you waiting for?

Your arrival has been anticipated for quite some time. For me, it began when your dad was about fifteen and I first started scheming to build a railroad track with a revolving train up along the ceiling of the living room in the house where we lived. I reasoned, even back then, that if I had that train running round and round, I would be the grandparent you would want to visit most when you came into the world one day.

Now, many years later, it is hard for me to really believe that you are almost here. Because I have anticipated your arrival for nearly two decades, my anxiousness is almost unbearable.

I am ready.

Since I learned from your mother and dad nine months ago that you were coming into our lives as my first grandchild, I have tried my very best to temper and pace my enthusiasm. That meant, among other things, not having a major fireworks show in the backyard to celebrate your coming when you were only two weeks known. I think that I, like so many people my age, worried that if I thought about you too much too soon, something might happen and you might never come.

But a couple of months ago when it appeared certain your birth was inevitable, I uncapped any cork that was remaining on my fervor. I have painted your room in my house a bright yellow and added a Winnie the Pooh border up top, Winnie stickers on the wall, a Winnie rug, Winnie bedding on your beautiful white bed, a Winnie mobile, a Winnie bed light, and a Winnie changing table and diaper bag. Piglet and Tigger sit around the room, and talking Winnie toys are everywhere. It now looks like a baby museum and a playroom for Winnie the Pooh and friends.

During the last month, I have taken many of my friends upstairs to marvel at your nursery. At night I go there alone and play with your toys and just think what it will be like when you visit. I dream of Saturday morning soccer games, school Christmas plays, the first fish you hook, and what it will be like to play catch, take walks, read books, and sing songs.

There is something very special in your room, hanging on the wall right behind the rocking chair. And when you get older I will tell you more about the big black-and-white photograph of your dad and me that was taken when he was about five years old. It was on July 4th, and we were sitting on the curb in downtown Jacksonville, watching the parade. For the last twenty-seven years it has always hung in my room. Now I want to share it with you. One day, you will notice that your dad has a photograph just like it.

Over the next months and years, I will write to you often, and in my letters I will talk to you about many things. Mostly, I will probably tell you how you have captured my days and nights and turned my own priorities upside down and right side up. I will use these letters to share stories I know and experiences I have had, and I will hope that somehow, because of them, you will better understand and love the world around you.

You are being born into a very special life, in a very special place, and during a very special time.

As your granddad, I want to help you to understand lots of stuff, including:

Your mom and dad love you, no matter what.

Family really is most important.

Life is not always fair, but we should always play fair.

The glass is always at least half full.

Life is relative, and when we complain about a sore toe, we should remember there are people with no feet.

We are responsible for our own lives, our own behavior, our own actions; when something goes bad, it is most often because of what we have done, not something others have done unto us.

When you get knocked down, get back up.

It is okay to say no; there is no shame in being wrong, but there is disgrace in doing nothing.

And the Golden Rule is right.

Of course, there will be other things you should know, and as a doting granddad with the wisdom of my years, I will most likely share them with you without hesitation.

Finally, sweet, yet-unborn Mack, I am most hopeful that you will grow up to be like your mom and dad. You could not come into this world to live with finer, more loving people.

Your mom may be tiny, but she is strong-willed and has the smile and kindness of a thousand angels. She is creative, curious, and quiet. Most important, she loves your dad in a way that is inspiring. One day, one of us will tell you the story about how the two of them broke up in college, and how after graduation your mom joined the Peace Corps and spent two years in South Africa.

Your dad is a funny guy who loves to laugh. There is just enough devilishness in his soul to keep us all, including your mom, on our toes. But he has always had a wonderful work ethic, and when he sets his mind on something, it gets done. He is smart, and when he reads you stories it will cause you to fall in love with literature. But what really sets your dad apart is a gentleness and a sweetness that causes most everyone he meets to like and admire him. He met your mom very early in their sophomore year in college, and from that first moment some ten years ago, he has been totally in love with her.

However, right now the two of them are tired of waiting on you to arrive. They are so eager to see you and hold you and take you home to your own room in your new house.

Remember how I told you that your dad is funny? Let me close with this little story. Over one year ago, I received a call at work from him and he asked if I was sitting down because he had something important he wanted to tell me. Well, I surely thought the news was going to be that the doctor had told him and your mom that little Mack was on the way to live with them. But that was not it.

Instead, he wanted to let me know that he and your mother had decided it was time for them to go looking for you, little Mack. He said that when they found you they were going to bring you home and love you and share you with me and with so many others who are looking forward to loving you as well.

And, so, sweet child, I sit here by the phone, waiting, with a beeper attached to each side of my pants, hoping that in the next near hours we will meet for the very first time.

Love,
Your granddad

—*Mike Tolbert*

The Indomitable
Miss Chelsea

Finding my finger clenched tightly in a tiny hand, I have no choice but to follow along behind my confident, though diminutive, leader. Platinum blonde curls kiss the top of her collar as she swivels her head from side to side, and I know her bright eyes aren't missing a thing. Her pink-socked feet barely leave depressions in the carpet, but she's so full of herself that her wee size doesn't matter. Thirteen-month-old Chelsea is in charge.

Our current destination is the breezy, screened front door, and I smile as she pats the wire, chattering to the dog watching from the porch. The dog wags her tail, and Chelsea jabbers something, then spins around and drags me back across the floor. She is a baby on a mission.

Next stop is the big, red, plastic bucket filled with toys. I laugh as Chelsea squats beside it and begins to toss things out, one item at a time. She flashes me a huge grin, a new tooth gleaming proudly on her bottom gum. She chooses a stacking toy, and seats herself on the floor. Clutching a colorful plastic ring in each hand, she reaches out her right arm and drops the first piece onto the pedestal. Then slowly, deliberately, she moves her left arm forward.

A familiar ache twists my heart as I watch Chelsea try unsuccessfully to make her stiff left arm and hand cooperate. Finally she solves the problem by taking the ring in her right hand and depositing it on the center stand. She turns her bright face up to mine, her eyes shining with happiness.

"Good job!" I cheer, clapping enthusiastically. She clasps her hands together and swings them back and forth, cheering with me. Then she removes the rings and starts all over again. Knowing that this game can go on for a while, I settle in to watch, applauding each time she successfully slips a ring in place.

My only granddaughter, Chelsea is the spitting image of my daughter, her mother, when she was the same age. It is hard to tell their baby pictures apart. They share identical blonde curls, round blue eyes, and perfect complexions. But there is something dramatically different about Chelsea, something that presents her with daily challenges that most of us never think about.

Chelsea has Erbs palsy, a condition that occurs as a result of an injury during childbirth to the brachial plexus nerve network. Babies with these injuries suffer various degrees of difficulty. Some infants recover spontaneously and never require so much as one round of physical therapy. Others are faced with multiple surgeries and reduced or, in some cases, no usage of the affected limbs. Unfortunately, Chelsea's case is one of the more serious.

She looked perfect in the first moments after she was born, but it soon became evident that things weren't so wonderful. Chelsea's left arm lay limp and motionless, not waving around like the other. A few hours later, her pediatrician called a family meeting and delivered the bad news. Chelsea had suffered a significant injury and might never use her arm.

After that heart-wrenching meeting, I wandered down to the nursery and stared through the window. I had no problem picking out my granddaughter from the other babies. At 10 pounds, 7 ounces, she was hard to miss; she was the biggest baby there. And there was the soft little sling wrapped around her injured arm, keeping it snuggled close to her body. Just the sight of it sent waves of sadness rushing through my soul.

The pediatrician's comments haunted me. He'd explained to the family that the injury would be more of a handicap to any of us than it ever would be for Chelsea, because she would never know anything different. I realized that what he said was true, but that didn't ease my pain or concern. *What problems would she face? Would she ever be able to do the things that babies usually do, like crawl or play patty-cake?* I grieved for my precious little granddaughter.

Otherwise extremely healthy, Chelsea had a loud, robust cry that seemed much louder than her older brother's had been and an angelic face that melted my heart. And as the early days passed, it became obvious that there would be no spontaneous recovery for her. The affected arm lay completely still, with no muscle tone at all. The little sling Chelsea wore barely kept it from shifting and hurting her, so we carefully propped it against a tiny pillow or a rolled-up blanket in the bassinet. I cradled her gently to avoid jarring it and tried not to let it drop suddenly when laying her down for a diaper change. It was scary learning how to do things right.

Then, just after she turned two months old, she began lifting her arm a tiny bit and rotating her wrist. Slowly, she gained strength and motion and began to show signs of recovery. I felt like I had won the lottery.

But then a rapid growth spurt caused her to grow several inches in a short period of time, and the nerves in her neck failed to grow at the same rate.

The muscles in her left arm stiffened, pulling her elbow into a bent position, and no matter how much we tried to gently straighten her arm, it would not relax.

The specialist was not encouraging. He even mentioned the possibility that Chelsea would never be able to turn her head from side to side and warned that the muscles in her arm could pull so severely that it might dislocate her shoulder. But he didn't know Chelsea. She fought it through, and the muscles began to relax, her arm moved more freely, and her head turned immediately toward any interesting sight or sound. She wasn't about to miss a thing!

Over the months, Chelsea endured uncomfortable braces (and figured ways out of each one), numerous visits to specialists, and physical therapy sessions that she didn't like one bit. Each time, she surprised everyone with her resilience and improvements.

She figured out how to pull herself along on her tummy, tucking her left arm safely out of the way. Though she looked awkward, her two older brothers learned not to be deceived by her strange movements. Chelsea would snatch their unattended toys as quick as a flash and then make a speedy getaway, leaving them wailing in surprise. When she started walking, she grasped her treasures securely in her left hand while she used her right to steady herself on pieces of furniture or the wall. Nothing slowed her down, and she compensated for the injured arm in creative, workable ways.

Even with these successes, Chelsea faces years of physical therapy, possible surgery, and lots of challenges. But she meets every day with confidence, enthusiasm, and good humor. Sure, her arm might cause her a little bit of inconvenience now and then, but she works around it. Not once has she complained or tried to use it as an excuse. She has too much to do.

These days she is busy leading her willing grammie around by the heartstrings. I follow wherever she goes, anxiously waiting to see what adventures we'll have next. And while I'm teaching her things like how to say "please" and "thank you," she's teaching me much bigger lessons—like never giving up, no matter what. When the problem looks insolvable, Chelsea finds a creative solution. And if that little girl can patiently and with good humor find ways around whatever roadblocks stand in her way, how can I let my so-called problems get me down? Lead on, Miss Chelsea, lead on!

—*Anne C. Watkins*

My Granddaughters, My Life

When my wife of fifty-nine years died, I could see no reason for living. I started to tie up loose ends and to get things in order so I wouldn't leave my sons with a disaster. Neighbors I had never met came ringing my doorbell with offers of help. I decided to take a trip from California to Rochester, New York, to say goodbye to my son and daughter-in-law and to my granddaughters. I had no idea of the effect that seeing the young girls again would have on me.

My older granddaughter was independent and reserved. I didn't see too much of her. She spent most of her time with her schoolwork and her friends. But the five-year-old twins greeted me with open arms. They would see me at the other end of the grocery store and come rushing to me, shouting, "Grandpapa!" While their mother was gathering groceries, they would put a bouquet of flowers in the cart for me.

Catherine Elizabeth and Heather Ann Langley are identical twins. They look and act so much alike that I couldn't understand how their parents told them apart. I'm certain that much of the time I called each of them by the wrong name, but they were too polite to correct me. Or maybe they thought that sharing identical DNA might as well extend to sharing names. Sharing a grandfather was one of the things they did best.

While I was visiting, the people who owned the house next to my son's moved to Florida and put their house up for sale. I bought it before a sign went up and then went back to California to sell my house there and prepare for moving.

Back in Rochester again, the twins spent much time with me. They came over with CDs or videos to listen to or watch with me, or brought books to read to me or have me read to them. They invited me to visit them in their preschool class and made certain all the other kids knew that I belonged to them. After that, I was often approached by some little one in a store or on the street who greeted me with, "Hello, Catherine and Heather's grandfather." It made me feel like a very important man.

When they came to visit Grandpa, they worked in tandem. The first one in piled pillows on my lap and climbed to the top to watch the entertainment; the other one inserted a CD or video and sat at my feet. Then they found that by piling a bean-bag cushion on me there was room for both of them up there. We ate popcorn or cheese and crackers, and they drank chocolate milk, which they insisted on making themselves. I would sip diet cola. I stocked my fridge with orange soda, because that was the only flavor they would drink. We watched the same videos over and over. I once asked Catherine how many times she thought we had seen *Cats*, and she answered, "About a thousand times." They knew the lyrics to all the songs, and when the worn tape left out bits of dialogue, they filled it in from memory. Heather managed to duplicate the difficult choreography she saw the frisky felines perform.

Once when they showed up, Heather carried sheets of paper in one hand and a ballpoint pen in the other.

"What are you doing?" I asked.

"I'm writing a book," she explained.

Knowing that they usually did things together, I asked Catherine, "Are you writing a book, too?"

"No," she answered sweetly, "I don't have the time. I'm too busy reading."

I knew then that we three shared hobbies that transcended the span of years between us.

The girls were just beginning to ride their bikes, and they would ring my doorbell and ask me if I wanted to watch them. When on rollerblades, they used me to stop by crashing into me and hanging on. That winter they made snow angels and built snowmen, and they grabbed big shovels to try to clear a path for me in the snow.

One day they had an announcement for their mother. "Grandpapa has so much room in his house that we think we will move in. But don't be sad, because we will visit you every day."

They discussed the upcoming move for several days. Then Catherine showed up without the ever-present smile on her pretty face.

"What's the matter?" I asked, "Is something wrong?"

"Daddy says we can't move. He says he needs us to tell him when his violin is out of tune when he practices."

She sat morose for a full minute, and then the smile began finding its way back to its usual place.

"But he said we could visit you anytime he isn't practicing," she added.

It was then that I decided life was still worth living and that my future, and the future of the entire universe, was in the skilled and adept hands of my grandtwins and of the other grandchildren all over the world.

Two years ago Catherine got sick at school. Her mother picked her up and took her to the doctor. He sent her to the hospital, where she was diagnosed with Hodgkin's disease, a form of cancer. They operated on her and removed the mass, then put her on chemotherapy. She lost her beautiful hair and wore a floppy hat given to her by her uncle. Her sisters designed a T-shirt with a butterfly and the logo, "Cat Will Soar to a Cure on Our Wings." The local television station picked up the story, and the entire community came forward to help. They threw a pasta dinner to raise funds for her treatment. Throughout the chemotherapy, she remained upbeat and kept up with her schoolwork. When the ordeal was over, she thanked her doctors and the nurses for "making it not so bad." She recently passed her one-year-after checkup with flying colors and is once again her vibrant self.

When I got word of her illness, it had a drastic effect on me. I tottered around for a few days on my cane, and then collapsed on the floor and was taken to the emergency room. My problem, I was told, was stress-related heart failure. After keeping me in the hospital for a week, my cardiologist decided I should go directly to a managed-care unit, as I was no longer able to take care of myself at home. My granddaughters are growing up fast and are involved with their schoolwork and their friends. Although I lived just two doors away, I seldom saw them. In a care unit, I felt I wouldn't see them at all, so I insisted on going home. Now I am able to do small things around the house, and I do my own cooking. But mostly, I sit and wait for a glimpse of the lights of my life.

—*Charles Langley*

Toy Box Confidential

I bend forward to collect the deserted toys scattered about like snoozing slackers. Moving Tommy activates friendly chatter: "Hi. I'm Tommy the Telephone. Anybody wanna play? *Ding-a-ling. Ding-a-ling.*"

No, Tommy. Not any time soon. I return verbose Tommy to his designated place in the toy box—next to his neighbors, the Littlest Pet Shop, the Scrambled Eggs and Boppin' Bee games, a red Etch-a-Sketch, a doctor's kit, and three puzzles with worn edges.

The box is a Wal-Mart special, a green plastic storage crate with a cream flip top and a handle at each end. The nondescript stand-in toy box, its only distinguishing feature a few sticky fingerprints, came out of the closet to bail four bubbling cherubs from the bondage of boredom at Grandma's house. For five years of serious fun, it served as a sentry for these playthings—except for a few pet shop critters that were "borrowed" with permission and lost their way home.

Over the years, it endured silly knock-knock jokes, which grew sillier with each retelling. It recorded a deluge of pricey desires from Lego's catalogs: "I'll take the Black Sea Barracuda . . . King Leo's Castle . . . Mars Exploration Rover."

It decoded whispered secrets so hush-hush they were inaudible to my ears: "Grandy, *pssst* and *shhh* can *whhhh* Saturday." The crate also served as a confessional: "I broke Mama's bowl, but I'm not in very bad trouble." It saw trivial arguments erupt and settle, and witnessed the Fascinating Four patrol each other with simple words: "Share." "Be nice." "Take turns." The box also knows the art of negotiation starts early. "If you let me go first this time, you can go first next time." "I'll trade my McDonald's Pluto for your Mickey Mouse." "Grandy, let's make a deal. If I eat my food, I get a Popsicle."

The grass-green box doubled as a battleground for action figures and witnessed a bunch of bad guys blown away in imaginary shoot-outs. One day it overheard a small, tentative voice ask, "Did Davy Crockett die at the Alamo?" "Yes. Sometimes, in real life, heroes die—even when defended by cannons, knives, and rifles and wearing a coonskin cap."

The rectangular box was there when a four-year-old made a shocking discovery, "Grandy, you have wrinkled elbows," and when she announced, "I can spell 'no' . . . n-o!" It shared a poignant holiday moment after a significant loss: "When I looked on the front door where we tape all our Christmas cards, Nana Gigi's wasn't there."

It watched confidence roll in with the turning of calendar pages: "I can do this Bee game now." "This parrot puzzle isn't hard anymore." It shared the miracle of miniature teeth that loosen, fall, and replace themselves after the fairy comes. With every falling fang, it heard the phone ring: "Grandy, I lost a tooth!" The mute box observed growing self-esteem when a granddaughter, cocking her head coyly, asked, "If they want you to star in a movie, do you have to do it?" and when her sister smiled into the mirror, admired her new orchid pajamas, and said, "I really look cool in these."

The box attests that being goofy is good for your health, that bruises heal faster with dinosaur Band-Aids, and that small people marvel at small things. "Grandy, you always remember where we live." It knows that the young are ungreedy at unexpected times, "The Christmas tree is my favorite part of Christmas. We don't need all those new toys, anyway."

The box knows grandkids can't injure a grandparent's feelings. "I saw a picture of you before you got old. You had long, blond hair." "How come when people get old like you, Grandy, their hair turns curly?" "Mama can really, really make better scrambled eggs than you." It watched a child charm a grandmother: "How come your food always tastes better than ours?" "You have the best grape juice ever."

It knows that children have purity of soul. I brushed the shiny, flowing hair and secured my granddaughter's ponytail. Eyes bright, voice merry, she said with solid sincerity, "When I am a Grandy and you are a little girl, I will help you get ready for ballet."

The box affirms that sharing simple pleasures makes precious memories.

Earlier today, the grandkids and I brought out the toy box for one last time. This playtime was less raucous than usual—in slow motion—as if we were paying unspoken tribute to the passing of something splendid. Mid-morning, a red, overloaded Suburban swept the four seraphs and their parents away to an out-of-state residence.

Tonight I feel a need to put away the toys, alone, slowly. Three puzzles—a parrot, a turtle, a clown— were put together one last time by innocent fingers. Maybe it's my imagination, but the clown's smiling face appears distressed as I place it in the box. The Etch-a-Sketch displays a creative design I dare not disturb. The life-saving doctor's kit that has examined small beating hearts, injected dreaded shots, detected soaring temperatures, and done surgery on make-believe frogs has no patients. The pet shop is closed for business.

I ask the green box, "Will these toys be covered in dust—or rust?" "Will you, too, long for the loving touch of tiny hands?"

My heart knows the answer. Our secrets are one.

I close the lid on the toy box and drag it to the back of the closet. The motion again displaces Tommy the Telephone. "Anybody wanna play? Everybody hold hands. *Ding-a-ling.*"

My gaze lingers on the bright-green plastic crate. Longfellow was right: "Golden moments fly." I think I'll leave the fingerprints on it for a while. Somehow fingerprints make the distance from Texas to Arizona seem much shorter.

—*Darla Curry*

How Do I Love Thee?

"How do I love thee? / Let me count the ways. . . ."

My apologies to Elizabeth Barrett Browning for exploiting her beautiful words, and, yes, I know she had a lover in mind, not a child, when she penned that soulful poem. But love comes in many forms, and her eloquent words could just as easily apply to the love of a grandparent for a grandchild.

In fact, the relationship between grandparents and grandchildren is often quite special . . . and unique—so much so that it can baffle those who are not yet grandparents themselves. Take, for example, the people who wonder at how differently their parents treated them from the way they treat their grandchildren. Maybe it's because grandparents have fewer responsibilities than they did when they were raising children and so can devote more attention to the grandchildren. Perhaps it's because they were inexperienced as parents, and by the time they've become grandparents, they have gained more understanding and a different perspective. Or it might simply be that after a day of fun and hugs, grandparents can send the kids home to their parents, knowing it is their turn to handle the challenging stuff.

But when push comes to shove, when the going gets tough, just how strong is a grandparent's love for a grandchild? Let me try to answer that by relating my experience as a first-time grandmother.

Recently, my daughter came to visit from out of town with her three-year-old son, Ronnie, in tow. This high-maintenance ball of energy would rise at about 7:00 A.M. each morning and find his way to Grandma and Grandpa's bedroom.

With his little cherub face two inches from my still-sleeping one, he'd whisper, "Wake up! It's a boodifu day."

I'd gaze sleepily into a pair of dark eyes peering at me from under long, dark, curly lashes framing a peaches-and-cream complexion topped by a mass of dark hair.

"Let's play," he'd urge.

So the day would begin. It would continue nonstop—play, play, play—without the requisite nap—mine—until about 9:30 P.M.

Because Ronnie is our first and only grandchild, play items at our house are few, and those we do have are leftovers from his mother's childhood. So one day we went shopping for some badly needed supplies. After choosing a few items, we were about to leave the store when he spotted a small, bright yellow helicopter in a shiny box. He was so enamored with this "copta" that he was prepared to give up everything else he had chosen. What could we do? Isn't spoiling grandchildren our job and our constitutional right? We had no choice but to add the little yellow aircraft with its four black rotors on top to our purchases. It was just the right size for his small hand, and he held it tightly all the way home. He even ate with it and slept with it.

A few days later, Ronnie and I were playing a game, and he declared, "I have to go poo."

"Okay, hon," I said. "I know you're a big boy now and can go by yourself."

Off he scurried to the bathroom. While he was doing his big-boy business, I began to prepare supper in the kitchen. His grandfather was watching golf on TV in the living room, and his mother was working on the computer in the den. Suddenly, the quiet was shattered by loud, explosive screams. From all quarters, everyone rushed to the bathroom in a panic. There was our little guy, sitting on the toilet, head in his hands, sobbing uncontrollably. We looked around. We looked at each other. We saw nothing.

"What's wrong, baby?" I asked.

His words were lost in a flood of tears, rendering them incomprehensible. Finally, between choking sobs, he managed to blubber, "'Copta in toilee."

I lifted him off the toilet seat and looked inside. Sure enough, the little yellow helicopter was floating in a sea of yellow pee with dollops of brown doo-doo dotting the watery landscape. I instantly understood the source of his anguish; he thought his most precious possession was about to be sucked down into the dark netherworld. He was crying so hard, he seemed to be drowning in tears. In a flash, before it could slip away, I plunged my hand into the foul soup and scooped out the hapless "copta." Ronnie's eyes and mouth opened wide with surprise and wonder. Then he uttered a squeal of delight and relief, and his face melted into a smile. While I held the valuable, if repugnant, commodity dripping over the bowl, the tension broke and howls of laughter erupted in the crowded room. The crisis over, I was dubbed a rescue hero, though it's usually helicopters that rescue people.

Needless to say, we thoroughly disinfected both the toy and Grandma. Peace and calm—punctuated, of course, by the happy sounds of a lively, carefree toddler—returned to the household. And it was then that I knew the depths to which I would go for my grandson.

On a return visit to my daughter's home in another part of the country, I decided to take my grandson, now four years old, to a local fast food chain that had a play place. I had taken him there on a previous visit, and he had loved it, climbing all over the structure and sliding through the tubes with confidence and delight. This time, though he was older, bigger, stronger, and more coordinated, he was reluctant and fearful. I didn't understand what had caused the change, but no amount of urging could persuade him to climb into the cavernous enclosure. Finally, after much coaxing and encouragement and reminders of how much fun he'd had before, he dared to enter. I quickly came to regret that, when a pitiful cry rang out from above.

I looked up to see Ronnie on the fourth level, suspended on all fours atop a webbed climbing bridge, staring down with a look of wild panic in his eyes. He made no further sound, but his face was a mask of sheer terror as he clung to the mesh with his fingers, his sturdy little body stretched across the unsteady strands, frozen to the spot. At first I thought one of his toes or feet might have gotten tangled in the netting, but that was not the case. A young male employee stood uselessly, contemplating a course of action, and then left to consult with his manager. I had no choice. I scrambled up the wobbly webbing all the way to the fourth level, and Ronnie finally let go to tightly grasp my outstretched arms. I felt every ounce of his full, hefty weight as I lifted him, but I held fast and was able to bring him down safely without incident.

Only afterward did I visualize how I must have looked to all the young parents sitting in the area who witnessed the scene: a petite, seventy-year-old grandmother propelling herself up the structure faster than any of their offspring, plucking a hefty four-year-old off the netting, and carrying him down four levels without so much as a waver. In the calm aftermath, I was surprised and secretly proud of how quick, agile, and strong I still was.

It was then that I realized the heights to which I'd go for my grandson.

So if the next Grandma challenge finds me paddling a canoe across an ocean, I can truthfully answer, "I love thee to the depth and breadth and height my soul can reach"—just like the poem.

—*Libby Simon*

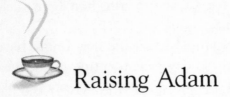 Raising Adam

Do you think he's delusional too?" The social worker's question took me aback, it was blunt to the point of cruelty, but then that was her style.

"Do you mean like his mother?" His mother, my daughter. "No. I think he's been living in her world and trying to cope with it. Her reality has been all that he's known."

"All he talks about is clues. The streetlights are clues. The cracks in the sidewalk are clues. That is not normal."

She was right, but what could be normal living with a mentally ill mother? The social worker shook her head and slid the papers across the table for me to sign. I could see she'd rather commit Adam to an institution than let him live with me. In big, bold letters, she'd written, "Emotionally disabled, physically violent."

I signed quickly, pretending to myself that I wasn't terrified—for him and for me. He was five and a half; I was fifty-five. I'd be seventy when he was twenty. *What if I couldn't help him, couldn't handle his aggression, couldn't protect myself?* But there wasn't another choice. Foster homes wouldn't accept him. Without me, he'd live a nomadic life being passed from one group home to another, devoid of help and hope.

It would have been easier if they had removed him from her custody sooner, but I hadn't had proof. For his first three years, she shared her paranoia with me but was still enough in control to hide it from the authorities. Even when she began to reveal it to others, they didn't seem interested in pursuing a case of neglect. She loved her son, but wrapped up in a world filled with secret messages in junk mail and invisible cameras hidden in walls, she couldn't take care of him. Nothing was done until she'd refused to enroll him in school and kept him locked inside her apartment so he couldn't be "kidnapped." He was already six months behind academically and three years behind in social skills.

I should have been jubilant that they'd finally listened, that I'd finally won. I wasn't. I was angry, depressed, and I needed to cry. That would have to wait. First I had to pack away my breakables. I'd disliked childproofing my house as a young mother and hated it now. It wasn't fair. I'd waited years to own things I loved. Even before the delusions started, I'd begged her not to have a child. Both she and her boyfriend were using street drugs. They were too irresponsible to take care of themselves, let alone a baby. They didn't listen, castigating me because I wouldn't support their decision. A few months later, she was pregnant. Three months after his birth, my grandson's father left, flying north to escape the pressures of parenthood. Just as I'd feared, I'd ended up raising their child at an age when I deserved other pursuits: travel, indulgence, adventure. As I wrapped my beloved sculptures in tissue paper, I wondered when I'd see them again. It felt like never.

Raising a five-year-old with two-year-old social skills would be hard enough. It could only get worse when he reached eight, ten, fifteen. It wasn't long before I found myself sitting across the room from a children's therapist. "Then don't tell him 'no,'" she said. At first, I wasn't sure I'd heard correctly, but she went on. "If 'no' is the trigger for his violence, you have to avoid using that word." The amazement on my face must have encouraged her. "Use euphemisms instead; phrases that mean 'no' but don't directly say it."

I left wondering who the delusional party was. Later, as I worked with one of my horses, I pondered her words. For twenty years I'd taught kids to ride, and a primary tenet of my teaching was that their words must be clear and firm if they expected a horse to

understand: "Whoa" always had to mean "Stop immediately and don't move." "Walk" always had to mean
"walk" and never "trot," "canter," or "whoa." People are
the same. When someone says "sheep" to us, we immediately conjure a mental picture of that animal, because
the word always means the same thing. How could my
grandson learn the solidity of words if I wasn't to speak
them and reinforce their meaning?

I searched the house for anything that could be
used as a weapon. Kitchen knives, tools, and baseball
bats were locked up. I placed a blanket and reading
material in each room. The next time I said 'no' and
he rushed at me—raging, hitting, kicking—I was
prepared. He soon found himself on the carpet, all
extremities securely wrapped and harmless, while
I held him down. As soon as I was sure I was in
control, I picked up my book and feigned reading.
At first he howled louder, but then he tired and quit
struggling. As I continued to read, he tried to get my
attention with more screaming and struggling, but
then tired again. When he began to cry, I put down
the book and held him close. This was the first step
toward learning that violence earned nothing and
sharing other emotions was worthy of attention.

The therapist agreed with the social worker—he
was delusional. She cited his sometimes meaningless
chatter, wide-ranging imagination, and insistence
on looking for clues. But these were symptoms and

analyses based on words. His words obviously contained different meanings for him than they did for us. This was his language of love—mother's love, his love, the agony in his heart as he struggled to understand her ramblings. With her, words weren't solid; he had to guess their meaning anew each time she uttered them. His agony was a shared agony. I, too, didn't understand her, yet I loved her and missed her, and I knew my love didn't have the power to heal her. Sometimes we cried together.

Kindergarten went better than I expected. Academically, he was closing the gap quickly. Though he didn't rage at school, he didn't know how to play with the other children. He spent most of recess sitting on the bench, talking to his teacher. She was kind when she called. "The other kids don't understand what he's talking about. They think he's strange. Maybe you should teach him not to share those ideas when he's here."

We were back to words. Shared words must have a frame of reference. His didn't. He didn't know what a swing or slide was, didn't know the rules for kick ball, had never seen the most popular movies, and had never touched the most popular toys. I set out to expand his world. Renting movies and buying toys was the easy part. They kept him entertained for hours.

The harder part was controlling him in public. Crossing a parking lot became a nightmare as he tried to dash away, oblivious to the danger. Going to the park was equally frightening. As soon as I let go of his hand, he ran and ran, without looking back. I gave chase but fell behind. A fence at the other end of the 200-acre expanse was all that stopped him. It soon became apparent that any large place was too much excitement. I spent a half-hour searching through a large department store, only to find him huddled behind a display of hanging rugs. He was angry I hadn't rescued him sooner. After that, his favorite word became 'no.' No, he didn't want to go shopping. No, he didn't want to play on the beach, walk on the pier, or ride a merry-go-round. No, he didn't trust the world beyond the front door.

It didn't help that I was an introvert, content to spend my hours alone and silent with my books, animals, and garden. I didn't relish joining the young mothers at the park who chatted as their children played. I felt out of place and out of time. That experience belonged to a younger era I didn't want to repeat.

The new therapist was reassuring. "This is perfectly normal for someone living their life out of sequence. It causes a feeling of disorientation. You need to keep your life today on track at the same time you revisit the things you did in your twenties while raising your daughters."

Equally troubling was my resentment. I envied other grandmothers who got to spoil their grandchildren and then send them home. I wanted to show him Disneyland or take him whale watching. I longed to be alone in my bed, but he was terrified to sleep in his own room, because Mom had taught him strangers were outside waiting to break the window and kidnap him. I hated the added laundry, nagging about homework, and fighting over baths.

The new therapist understood. "Don't give up your world for his. Be who you want to be and bring him into that world. You'll both be happier."

Reading was too difficult. He lacked the patience and the ability to focus. His need for constant motion was distracting and frustrated me. So I started by clearing out a planter and giving it to him. He picked out seedlings at the nursery and found miniature statues of children at play in the garden center. The arrangement was his own, as was the satisfaction when the sweet peas and marigolds began to bloom. He held earthworms for the first time and was amazed we could buy ladybugs to control the aphids. He then found the web spun behind his plants and the one who decided the spider could stay. Ever driven by anxiety, the magic of the garden was the first to slow his frantic pace.

The animals were next. They needed few words and thrived on physical expression. The cats didn't tolerate rough play and he sported scratches to prove it, but he soon learned to tempt them with feathers on a string. The dogs sometimes played too rough, knocking him down more than once, but they offered adoration in return for tossing a ball. I stopped him from sitting on their backs and took him to the stable instead. The horses required more discipline. The old trainer called "Grandma" made him learn all the things hundreds of other children had also protested. "Safety first" was a motto he ignored until a careless hoof landed on top of his foot. Caution finally became part of his routine.

Only then did I tell him about the scaredy-cat. Spanky was the lone survivor of a litter of four. Their wild mother disappeared before they were weaned. I'd found the other kittens homes, but Spanky was terrified of everyone but me. He hid in my closet, coming out only at night after my grandson was asleep. He'd jump up beside me and stretch out on my left side, while my grandson slept on my right.

The night of their first meeting, my grandson feigned sleep until Spanky had settled, and then ever so slowly he reached across and scratched the fur behind Spanky's ears. Spanky purred until he realized it wasn't me, and then he fled. Thus began a long process, first establishing themselves as friendly acquaintances and then as true friends, but the rules never changed: I must be the buffer between.

Spanky's rules were my grandson's path to accepting the conventions of life. He began to realize that some rules were worth following because of the rewards reaped. I found that explaining the rules before an excursion helped. Our first overnight stay was in Long Beach. We visited the aquarium on Saturday and Ports o' Call on Sunday. Saturday was spent petting sharks and manta rays; Sunday found him at the helm next to the captain as we sailed around the harbor on a tall ship. I may not have brought him into the world, but I was finally having fun letting him show it to me.

My grandson is nine now. His unnatural fears are gone, replaced by an extraordinary boldness. He has the words to write vivid stories and a dream of being class president, plus the gentleness to comfort a lost soul. We still clash at times, but these conflicts are an ordinary part of growing up. What we share is far more important: love and spiritual blessings expressed through the divine rhythm of nature.

Watching him bloom gives me a special satisfaction. I still worry what the future will bring. *Can I handle the teen years? What will I do if my health fails?* But my confidence has blossomed alongside his progress. His growing happiness tells me I'm doing okay—that we're okay. What is more important than that?

—Miriya Kilmore

Adam is a pseudonym used in this story to protect the privacy of a minor.

How to Spoil a Grandchild and Alienate a Daughter-in-Law in One Easy Lesson

Dear Daughter-in-law:

I am very upset about your latest e-mail, and I really don't understand your negative attitude. I have made every effort to be helpful and offer suggestions about my grandchild that I think will be useful. I'm very sorry about the misunderstanding when I criticized your breastfeeding techniques. I know it isn't your fault, but really, dear, don't you believe you could try a bit harder? After all, it is only natural, and mothers all over the world do it without any trouble. So why can't you?

I'm also sorry about the remark I made about using disposable diapers instead of the old-fashioned kind. But those paper ones do remind me of a Kleenex, and the cloth ones were always good enough for my kids. Parents nowadays are really just too lazy to wash diapers.

I'm sorry that you didn't like the little T-shirts and burping pads that I gave you as a shower gift. I know you wanted the layette with the little angels, but, dear, we do need to be practical. I also don't understand why you are so mad about the nice Christmas gifts I gave my grandchild. The fact that they were better than what Santa could afford and made Santa look cheap is not my fault.

I hope by now you are rid of the filthy dog so the baby does not catch any dog germs from it. Also, that cat needs to go. It will jump in the bassinet and smother the baby. Didn't anyone ever tell you not to have a cat around a baby? I don't know why you want pets, anyhow. You have a child. That's enough.

I hope you are using the nursery monitor I gave you and have installed the electrical outlet guards and the safety locks. You can't be too careful these days, and we wouldn't want anything bad to happen because you are not being careful enough, would we? Also, be sure to keep that syrup of ipecac in the bathroom in case of accidental poisoning. It always pays to keep some on hand—believe me, I know.

Also, if you would rub the baby's chest with menthol salve, like I told you, he wouldn't be sick all the time. If you want my opinion, I think you should take the baby to my doctor for a good checkup instead of to that fancy pediatrician your doctor referred you to.

I don't know why you want me to quit buying clothes for my grandchild. I know you like to pick out the baby's clothes, but the ones I pick out are much nicer than anything you can afford. Also, I've found some fabulous thrift stores with baby things for next to nothing. Why waste your money?

I know the bicycle, baseball glove, and computer I bought may be a bit too advanced for a newborn, but the child will grow faster than you think. Grandparents need to be able to indulge themselves a bit for their first grandchild.

I hope you liked the baby and childcare books that I bought and also the subscription to the parenting magazine. They have all kinds of useful information for inexperienced parents. I still can't understand why you refuse to go to parenting classes.

Are you still upset about me coming over during the baby's naptime and waking him up the other day? I just wanted to see him, and I did hold him and rock him the whole time I was there to keep him from fussing. Probably the reason he is so fussy is that he is teething. Did you try whiskey on his gums like I told you?

I'm sorry I couldn't babysit the other day while you went to the doctor, but you were so upset when I rearranged the furniture to make the house child-proof that I didn't feel up to coming back for a while. Actually, I'm thinking of making a nursery at my place in the spare room. Then you can bring him over here, where he will be taken care of properly while you are out running around.

Are you remembering to change the baby's diaper frequently and give him a bath every day? You don't mind me asking, do you? It isn't that you are not a good mother, dear; it is just that I don't want the baby to get rashes or diseases from being dirty.

I've been thinking that perhaps you just have more than you can do. So I've decided to move in with you and take over to help out. No need to thank me, dear.

Love,
Mom

—Sheila Moss

The Flavors of the Mix

One evening last winter, my grandson and I sat by the side of the pool at the East Boulder Recreation Center, waiting for his swimming class to begin, sharing a box of animal crackers. He was in the tadpole group. He shivered, cold from the shower, and pulled the Winnie the Pooh towel tighter around his shoulders. I lifted him into my lap and hugged him. We looked up at the moon, a crescent, framed by the skylight. The sparkling water sent rippled reflections around the room. The sounds of laughter and splashing bounced off the green- and blue-speckled tile until it circled back around on itself, making it hard to distinguish individual sounds. I had to put my face close to his mouth to hear him speak.

"There's a new girl in school," he said. "Rosamaria." He trilled the first R and tapped the second one.

I told him that was a pretty name. He nodded and considered the lion cookie he held in his fist. He bit off its head.

"You can't make fun of her just because she's new," he said. He looked up at me, his brown eyes earnest, rimmed with lashes so thick and long my daughter jokes that she's going to trim them before he becomes a teenager, to save little girls' hearts.

Rosamaria, he told me, was nice. She was from Mexico and still didn't speak very much English. She had a pretty smile.

I saw Rosamaria's smile on Valentine's Day when I picked up my grandson from kindergarten. Children gathered in clusters, their voices loud, fueled by the excitement of the party and all that extra sugar. He sat in the back surrounded by three dark-haired girls. I threaded my way through the thigh-high tables. A chunky girl with blunt-cut, shoulder-length hair held back by two pink barrettes fed him candy hearts. He opened his mouth and shut his eyes. She slipped the candy on his tongue. He closed his lips and chewed.

"Ready to go?" I asked. He jumped up and launched himself at me, nearly knocking me down. He wrapped his arms around my neck. His soft lips brushed my cheek. He led me to his cubby by the front door. He pulled on his Colorado Rockies jacket, shiny purple and black, fraying at the cuffs. He showed me his backpack full of papers and valentines; then he raised his finger in the air and motioned me to wait. He fished around in his pack and pulled out a smashed, half-eaten peanut butter and jelly sandwich that had been hastily rewrapped in plastic by five-year-old hands. Thumping on sneakers that lit up with each step, he ran to the back of the room.

Two of the girls giggled. The chunky one smiled. Dimples framed her curved lips. He held the sandwich out to her. She took it in her hands and looked at it. She raised her eyebrows into a question mark.

As we walked to the car I asked him who that little girl was.

"Rosamaria," he said. He tucked his hand in mine.

My grandson visits us on Saturdays. He likes to play in his grandpa's studio. He wears one of Grandpa's old T-shirts. It falls to his calves and protects his clothes from the clay. He fashions small pieces: mostly sharks and dinosaurs. When they get hungry, he and Grandpa pretend to sneak into the kitchen.

"Let's steal some of your grandma's cookies," Grandpa fake-whispers.

The little boy looks like his father. He has his dad's dark shiny hair and smooth coffee skin but big eyes like his mother's. His face muscles quiver as he tries to hold in all the excitement he feels just to be alive. He nods, and Grandson and Grandpa tiptoe to the Cheshire cat cookie jar that sits on the counter. I hear the jar lid open.

"Grandma makes the best cookies in the whole world." My grandson forgets to whisper.

I don't laugh out loud. I sit at the dining room table, pretending to read, marking up pages with my green pen.

When my grandson came over last Saturday, we discovered the cookie jar was empty.

"I'm six now," he said. "That's big enough to make cookies."

I asked him which kind we should make as I pulled the flour, sugar, and vanilla off the shelf. His finger rested on his chin as he considered the possibilities.

"Peanut butter cookies are Grandpa's favorite," he said.

He pulled a wooden chair from beside the kitchen door to the counter and climbed up on it. I let him use the hand beater. As he mixed, the light brown and yellow swirled. The creamy peanut butter, chunky yellow butter, and grainy brown sugar, as sweet as first kisses, melded into a new form. He broke the egg, the product of two things joined. I explained that the egg provided the lightness that would hold the flavors together. I picked out the pieces of eggshell before he dumped in the flour, the everyday ingredient that gives the mix its substance.

Flour flew out of the bowl as he stirred. It dusted his arms and the front of his shirt.

"Rosamaria doesn't love me," he said. He let the spoon fall. I looked at his face. His brown eyes floated, lost.

He told me that he'd told Rosamaria he loved her at lunch that week. I pictured it: the gym filled with a hundred other kids squirming and yelling, the two of them sitting side by side in their little chairs at the back table under the American flag. I imagined him, holding a chicken nugget in his hand as he professed his love, pushing around his cut-up carrots and peas with a plastic fork afterwards.

"She says we can be friends." His lip trembled. He blinked his eyes and looked down at his hiking boots.

I kissed the top of his head and then, because I couldn't help it, rubbed my sagging cheek against his smooth one. "I love you, Bumbo," I whispered. I squeezed his hand.

"I know, but . . . " He looked down. His eyelashes rested on his cheekbones. A tear plopped into the cookie dough.

How could I tell him this will happen again and again? How could I tell him that even if he thinks he has it right, he can get complacent and it can still go wrong?

In the summer of our seventh year together, his grandfather and I almost fell apart. First we quit dancing around the kitchen floor; then we quit touching as we passed each other in the hall; then we quit talking. We edged around each other in our small house. If he said "yes," I thought *no*. If he moved high, I moved low. When he looked at me, his eyes held a quiet question that neither of us had the courage to put into words. The air between us was heavy and unclean. Finally, he left for a camping trip alone to sort out his thoughts.

The day he left, I spent over a hundred dollars on little jars: anti-wrinkle creams with labels that promised to make the years I've lived null and void, exfoliates that vowed to remove the damaged cells and reveal the fresh new skin underneath, gels for erasing stretch marks and cellulite, and bleaches for hiding the fuzz growing on my upper lip. When I put all of them on, I smelled like a funeral home. I rinsed off everything, scrubbed with a loofah, and threw the jars into the trash.

When his grandfather came back, my husband's full lips formed the words he needed to say. "I had to imagine life without you." His eyes looked five years old, big and hurt. I nodded that I knew and asked him how that was. He shook his head *no*. We sat together on the couch, twining our fingers, sharing the air made light again, and began the hard conversations that adjust the flavors of the mix.

My grandson doesn't know that his life almost changed that summer. I looked at him standing on the kitchen chair in a shaft of sunlight, his lip tucked under his new adult teeth, too big for his baby face. I wrapped plastic over the green bowl and explained that we had to let the dough chill. If you try to bake it too soon, it doesn't hold its shape. He gazed out the window through the red curtains. He brightened, lifted his head.

"I know," he said. He raised his little finger in the air like a light bulb that signaled a new idea. His whole face lit up.

"I'll paint her a beautiful picture!" I wanted to wrap him in my arms and hold him there forever.

—*Sydney Argenta*

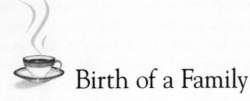

Birth of a Family

Baby Jacob has shaped my thoughts for months now. I've felt his mother, Tara's, swollen belly as his elbow or foot created a pulsing bulge, admired the ultrasound photo revealing his obvious masculinity, and planned my calendar around the possible day of his birth, which I've been invited to witness. I can't wait to run my finger along his cheek, which will surely be warm and smooth and soft as cashmere. It won't be long now. But my excitement is laced with worry as I stand in the doorway of the birthing room with my husband, Ray, who is Tara's father, and see my beloved stepdaughter struggling so hard to birth little Jacob.

A translucent green oxygen mask covers Tara's nose and mouth, a blood pressure cuff encircles her arm, and cords run from somewhere under her pink hospital gown to a beeping machine displaying her blood pressure, contractions, and the baby's heartbeat.

An IV drips pitocin to induce labor and magnesium to combat high blood pressure, which is so serious it is impairing liver and kidney function and could impede oxygen to the baby. I want to rush to her side and smooth her dark hair from her face.

I feel close to Tara. She lived with us summers while she went to college. She included me in many activities of her wedding day, and shares confidences and dreams with me when she visits. But just what is a stepmother's role in a situation like this?

Tara's mother, Donna, is already at her side, talking with her. She is facing Tara's health crisis without the support of her husband, Mike, who is at work. Tensions between Donna and Ray still crackle to the point that once we found it necessary to block her number on our phone.

Jared, Jacob's father, stands at the foot of the bed. Although we are very fond of each other, I wonder whether he might like to be alone with his wife at this intimate and important time, the birth of their first child.

Leana and Dave, Jared's parents, sit on a little sofa along the far wall. I have thoroughly enjoyed them on the few occasions we've gotten together. *Still, I worry, will they feel a stepmother is an intrusion on sacred family time?*

"Hi, Dad. Hi, Sam," Tara's voice is muffled by the oxygen mask.

"Hi," Donna turns to us and echoes Tara's greeting with a smile.

The smile helps a little bit. I take a deep breath and walk toward Tara's bed. Let's see. A stepmother is supposed to be eternally cheerful and supportive of everyone. Hopefully, I'm up to the challenge.

Ray squeezes Tara's hand. I bend and kiss her forehead.

"It's good to see you here," Jared says and wraps me in a warm hug.

His eyes reveal his concern for Tara and their unborn child. He probably expected to be walking the halls of this small hospital in Corvallis, Oregon, with Tara right now, enjoying panoramas of fields and woods seen through the large windows. Or perhaps rubbing her back and shoulders as she lies in a bath in the Jacuzzi provided as part of the birthing room, listening to the soothing music of Enya that they have brought along. Or coaching her as she experiments with different positions. Thirteen months earlier they were in this very hospital after Tara had miscarried with her first pregnancy. After that rocky road, today should have been a smooth one.

"They're worried about her kidneys and liver," Donna whispers in my ear.

Donna is prone to negativity, and I try to shush her instantly with my soft reply: "Yes, we know." In the next moment, my heart softens with sympathy for her. It is her youngest child lying so ill. "She's getting wonderful medical care," I say more gently to reassure us all.

Dave tells us that he's leaving to get a cup of coffee and hang out in the lounge for a while.

"He isn't comfortable being here," Leana quietly explains, then excuses herself to join him.

A wave of my own discomfort washes over me. He belongs here a lot more than I do.

A doctor comes in to break Tara's water. The greenish-black fluid indicates meconium that Jacob has expelled in utero. When he is born and takes his first breath, if he breathes it in, he can get pneumonia. There is, even at this time, a danger of infection.

"Everything will be fine," Jared says to Tara.

I hope he is a prophet. I inhale deeply and breathe out fear from the middle of my chest. Ray and Donna are both making small, worried noises. I take Ray's hand and hold it, pat Donna's arm, remind us all again of what good care the hospital is providing.

The doctor attempts to insert an instrument into Tara's uterus that will suction out the meconium, but she can't get past Jacob's head. Her efforts to place an internal monitor on Jacob are similarly blocked and cause Tara such pain that she gasps and claws at Jared's shirt.

"Look in my eyes, hon," Jared says. "Take deep breaths."

The doctor talks intently to all of us. When Tara is delivering, she will need to push out only the head, then pause while a pediatrician suctions out the baby's lungs. After he is born, the pediatrician will immediately suction the lungs again and give any other medical assistance required.

I want desperately to help in some way. Tara asks for ice chips, and I scurry across the hall to get them. Donna follows me, asking frantic questions to which I can't possibly know the answers. I put ice and water in a cup and hand it to her. "This is for you," I say. I fix ice water for Ray as well, and then take the ice chips to Tara. It's a hard time for us all.

Once the water is broken, the contractions come with ferocious frequency and intensity. Jared breathes with Tara through them. Still, Tara is not dilating as expected.

She agrees to an epidural for pain as long as she can feel the contractions enough to push when the time comes. Ray takes his cell phone into the hall to field calls to and from concerned siblings. I try to read, but it's difficult to concentrate. I get more ice for Tara, take little walks around the hospital with Ray, have lunch with Dave and Leana. We invite Donna, but she declines.

It is 6:00 P.M. Tara was admitted at 6:00 A.M. The doctor suggests a Cesarean section. I press my lips against a groan, thinking how disappointed Tara will be. Ray shakes his head. Tara, who has accepted everything else with grace, pleads for one more hour. The doctor reluctantly agrees. The hour creeps by, everyone silent, absorbed. When Tara is next checked she has progressed almost two centimeters, and everyone whoops with joy. Now things can click along.

"Get the mirror ready," Tara says. "I want to see Jacob born."

By 10:00, it is time to push. A nurse pulls a curtain around Tara's bed. The men tactfully withdraw. *Should I step out the door with Ray?* But Tara delights me with an invitation for all three grandmothers to stay. "Three grandmothers." What thrilling words. Donna moves to stand beside me on Tara's right. Jared is at her left. Leana arranges the full-length mirror.

"How long will I be pushing?" Tara asks.

"Usually two to four hours," the doctor replies.

"Four hours?" Tara moans. "I can't do it."

The epidural has worn off, and she is in excruciating pain. I grimace, too, remembering the awful sensation of literally turning myself inside out as I pushed my own children into the world.

"You can do it, sweets," Jared says. "You'll be fine."

They look into each other's eyes, this lovely, loving young couple.

"I know," she says with a little smile. "I'm having Jacob."

Now excitement crackles in the room. Jared watches the monitor.

"Contraction coming," he tells Tara. "Whenever you're ready."

"Now," Tara says.

Donna, Jared, and I work as a team to lift her legs toward her belly and support them. Everyone counts together. One, two, three . . . On the count of ten we all exhale audibly as we put her legs gently back on the bed until the graph of contractions begins to rise steadily, unremittingly, again. Every time Tara pushes, the doctor and nurse look at each other as if surprised by her strength. "Wow. Good push," they say.

We of an older generation marvel at the work of the doctor who massages and stretches the opening with oils at every contraction rather than making an episiotomy. I marvel, too, that I'm part of it all.

An hour passes. We see a tiny gray spot appear and then disappear as quickly as it came.

"There he is," the doctor announces.

Now we are crying out with excitement at every contraction. "I see it! Oh look, it's getting bigger."

"He always goes back in," Tara sighs between contractions.

I've never seen anything like it. The spot grows to the size of a dime, then a quarter. It quits disappearing between contractions. A half-dollar. A dollar. A coaster under my teacup. The pediatrician is standing with us now. Four more nurses stand to one side, where a cart has been set up to give Jacob immediate care after his birth.

"A big push now. Stop as soon as I tell you." The doctor puts her fingers around the gray blob as Tara pushes. "Keep pushing, keep pushing," she says, and maneuvers Jacob's head into the world. "Now stop," she says, and relinquishes her position to the pediatrician, who suctions Jacob's lungs.

Jacob's head makes me think of a sideways ice cream cone with gray hair matted on top, and yet I've never seen anything so beautiful. The ears are perfectly formed, exactly the right size, flat against his head. The nose is tiny, pushed up just at the end like mine. *It can't look like mine,* I remind myself. But it does.

Tara is red-faced and holding her entire body rigid. She must feel like she is holding back a rolling car.

The pediatrician steps aside. The doctor is back in position. "Okay," she says.

And just like that, there Jacob is in the doctor's hands.

"Oh, look at him. He's so big!" Tara's voice is filled with inexplicable joy and pride. "Hi, baby."

"He's so perfect," Jared says, his voice reverent. "So completely perfect. You did it, sweetheart," he adds, bending to kiss Tara.

Baby Jacob is perfect. Weighing in at nine pounds, four ounces, he isn't even wrinkled like the other newborns I have seen. I take one look at him and fall in love in a way I've never loved before.

"It's like a family giving birth in the old days," Tara says.

Indeed. Participation in the birth of our grandson has, for the moment, dissolved all tensions, and we truly are one family.

—*Samantha Ducloux Waltz*

Nonna's Way

1914

Angela Irene Giani was born to an aristocratic northern Italian family. Independent and opinionated long before women dared to be so, she had a degree in fine art and spoke four languages. When her sister died in childbirth, she married her brother-in-law, Enrico DeBernardi, and became mother to her sister's two children, Marie and Dino. A year later, the family went to America to build a better life.

Rich no more, Nonna worked in the shirt factories of New York City. Nonno, my grandfather, worked as a common laborer on the docks, where he endured prejudice and beatings. They lived in a walk-up in Little Italy, and the children—my uncle and my mother—slept in steamer trunks in unheated rooms so cold that water froze in glasses.

On Sunday, she bathed and dressed herself and her children in the last of the fine clothes from the old country. Then they walked eight miles to Central Park, and she set up an easel. She began to sell her watercolor scenes of the Big Apple skyline, and she taught painting and Italian to rich people. Their savings finally sent them north to Branford, Connecticut, where they, indeed, found that better life.

1930s–'40s

My nonna was fifty-one years old when I was born, and for much of my childhood we lived in a house just down the hill from hers, in Branford, Connecticut.

She and I were the only early risers in our family. I'd stand at the bathroom window looking up the hill, spying, as children do, waiting for the daily ritual I knew by heart and often pantomimed. Just at sunrise, the squeak of the kitchen's screen door announced Nonna's appearance. Wrapped in a lavender chenille robe, her twin gray braids reaching to her waist, she would arc her face around the door and survey the morning through black beetle eyes. As she waited for her *caffé robusto* to boil, she'd chirp to a bird or two, call to whatever stray animal she was caring for, and then plunge her hand deep into her robe pocket. Out would come a paisley hankie. She'd blow two good honks into the silvery dawn and then disappear into the kitchen, now filled with the aroma of rich, strong coffee.

No matter the time or place, Nonna always had a hankie ready to whip out for any number of uses. She used her ever-ready hankie to dust off the portraits of her parents, testaments to Nonna's great artistic talent. As she gently brushed the dust from each beloved face, she would relate some story about them. She'd use a hankie to wipe off the old deck of cards we used to play slapjack. She never said a word about the marked corners I'd carefully crafted, and she always let me win, knowing that my conscience would prevail in the end. It did. Eventually, I tearfully confessed to cheating, as Nonna dabbed the teardrops from my eyes.

Whenever I needed a shoulder to cry on, Nonna would dry my tears with her hankie and bring out the garish, flowered, "just-for-two" tea and sympathy set. Over the years, we must have shared a thousand cups of tea while Nonna listened attentively to my woes—from "nobody likes me," to the painful end of a serious romance, to petty marital squabbles, and frustrations with growing children.

"Et's nota so bad," she'd say, whipping out her ever-ready paisley hankie. "I dry you eyes."

"Thanks," I'd whimper, already feeling better.

"You love-a-you Nonna, eh?" Her face would be right in front of mine.

"Big as the moon and two rainbows," I'd answer, throwing my arms around her and kissing her a hundred times.

1977

I watched as she came spryly down the plane ramp. At the sight of the familiar squaring-off of the shoulders, the left-right head movement, and finally the raising of the proud chin, my heart started beating wildly and my eyes brimmed with tears. *Mia Nonna*, now ninety-two, had come because my forty-two-year-old husband had recently died of a wrecked heart. The minute her eyes found mine, her smile painted the sun onto my gray palette and her hands reached out for me.

"Ezabell! My darling! *Cara bella!* Come to your nonna!"

I collapsed into her, completely forgetting my daughters. Her strong arms encircled me; I rested my head on her shoulder.

"Nonna," I whispered, choking back tears. "I am so glad you're here."

"Yes, your Nonna is here, and I have surprises." She stepped back and held me out for inspection. "Let me look at you. . . . Ah! Skin and bones. Poor li'l t'ing." She hugged me again.

"Now, where are my great grandchildren? Who is this? Erica? Shauna?"

The girls came close and buried their faces in her skirt. My two small daughters had met her only once before, when they were too little to remember. I'd spent my whole life completely loving her, smelling her violet perfume, listening to her enormous intellect, eating her delicious food—being filled to the brim with Nonna.

"*Avante!*" she said. "We go home now. Nonna will take care of everything."

The first thing she unpacked was her flowered apron.

"We go to the market," she announced as soon as she was settled.

Two hours later, minestrone was bubbling on the stove, and she and her great granddaughters were elbow-deep in cookie dough.

"We use only the best ingredients. Real butter, no imitation. You don't get fat from good food," she instructed. "Beat. Beat."

The childhood smells of my grandmother's kitchen now filled my house, breathing life back into us all: garlic, Parmesan cheese, parsley, oregano, saffron, coffee, sugar cookies. The children rolled and patted the dough, traced around their hands with butter knives, and carefully lifted their sugar hand cookies onto a waiting pan.

"Slow oven. Not to overcook," Nonna trumpeted. "Bring your chairs closer and watch. When they are just golden around the edge, your hands are done! Blow ten times, they cool, and you can eat. First, we make tea."

She was a whirlwind in the kitchen. Stirring the minestrone, checking the cookies, patting the children's heads, turning on the kettle, hugging me.

That night she told the girls scary Italian stories and put them to bed. She lay down with me on the big bed that seemed so empty, and we watched TV together. Before the evening news, I was gone, sleeping the sleep of the dead. When morning came, I could already smell coffee brewing and heard soft voices coming from the kitchen.

"Sure. Eat the cookie," she whispered. "Just a pinch."

"Nonna," my eldest quizzed. "Does God like sugar?"

"Of course!" she answered sotto voce. "He made it, didn't he? But everything in moderation. You can't eat a dozen cookies for breakfast, eh?"

Throughout the next few weeks, Nonna taught us all to live again. She had daily chats with the girls about their daddy. She listened to me cry a lot. Afternoons, we went on walks—forced marches, really. Lacing her arm in mine, she'd command, "One, two, three! All on the same foot!" And off we'd go, a parade of four, with Nonna whistling an Italian aria and two old whining mutts struggling to keep up.

We ran through each others' shadows. We admired flowers. We leaned back to gaze at the clouds and made up stories about their shapes.

And when grief threatened to strangle us, Nonna wound up the silly old mechanical monkey she'd brought with her—the same one she'd used to cheer me up when I was growing up. Now, as then, it hopped wildly all over the table, bashing its cymbals, until it fell to the floor, still bashing. Every time it went over the edge, we all doubled up with such side-aching laughter we thought we'd perish.

Life came flowing back into us, ushered on the wings of the soul of this tiny, erect, determined woman who underlined healing with tea, sympathy, kisses, laughter, and dozens of sugar cookies. When it was time for Nonna to return to her Florida bungalow, the tears would not stop.

1983

"When the candle eza out, eza out. Poof!"

That's how Nonna talked about death. Nothing soppy. Nothing sorrowful. Just poof!

Angela Irene Giani DeBernardi lived to be ninety-eight years old. She died as she had lived, with dignity and in charge. Poof.

I traveled from my home in Albuquerque, New Mexico, to be with her during her last days. Later, my Aunt Mimi and I cleared out Nonna's house. Mimi, my uncle's wife, and my grandparents had lived side by side in two Sarasota, Florida, bungalows, and Mimi had cared for both my grandparents unselfishly and devotedly for many years.

"She wanted you to have her things," my aunt said, as we crossed the lawn to the empty little house next door. "You were the closest to her."

As we entered, the familiar odors yanked hard at my heart: oil paints, saffron, garlic, dust, stale coffee. I felt such loss. Nonna was my teacher, my confidante, my irresistible magician. She was the preserver and imparter of our family history. Above all, she was a comforter, a wizard who turned fire-eating dragon problems into small scuttling mice.

I stood in the center of the small living room surrounded by her—her painting paraphernalia, an old dusty trunk brought from Italy before World War I, the myriad odds and ends of nearly 100 years of living. My aunt and I spent the day sorting, boxing, discarding, and deciding what I would take home. I kept most of it, unable to part with even the smallest trifle, because everything was connected in some way to a memory. I couldn't bear to open the trunk and sent it sealed. I hand-carried the best paintings and crated the rest. Several brown paper packages tied up with strings and memories got mailed the next day.

For three years, I couldn't even approach her things, which gathered dust on a low shelf in our garage. Then one lovely spring day, the time seemed right. I slowly opened the trunk. Inside was exquisite linen bedding appliquéd with mythological scenes of Pan, chosen by Nonna when she was a child. I ran my hand over the embroidered "AG" . . . *Angela Giani*. There were old books and exquisite linen blazers covered with intricate cut work. A note in Nonna's script read: Lace from the 14th century, Florence, Italy, cathedral. There were elegant hand-embroidered tablecloths and napkins with pulled thread work and boxes of handkerchiefs. Some were silk; some were misty cotton; some had my great grandparents' initials; some were crocheted with rainbow scallops; and some were the undistinguished paisley ones I'd so often watched her use to blow her wonderful beak of a nose. And there was the ridiculous toy monkey.

After hand-washing everything, I had the appliquéd pillow cases, the antique lace, and the drawn-thread napkins sealed in acid-free frames. The old books went to lead-free boxes. I hung the beautiful cut-work blazers in my closet and still wear them for special occasions, usually collecting enormous interest that require the full story. I filled the fancier hankies with dried herbs and placed them in cupboards to sweeten linens. The paisley hankies went into the pockets of my robes.

2005

Four years ago, my eldest granddaughter, at seventeen, was diagnosed with non-Hodgkin's lymphoma. Four months ago, after endless hospitalizations, heartbreaking setbacks, terrible predictions, radiation treatments, chemotherapy, and two torturous bone-marrow transplants, after losing her magnificent red hair and enduring more suffering than anyone should ever have to bear, she became cancer-free. Throughout the 202 agonizing days of treatment, Nonna walked every step with me. I knew when to take over, when to back off, when to listen, when to make laughter, and when to comfort this suffering, beautiful child. At times I despaired that she might not make the next day, but I rode on the wings of Nonna's soul and kept breathing life into her.

Afterward, in my home, I'd look at Nonna's paintings, remembering and gathering strength. For two decades, her portraits have hung on our walls, giving honor to our family and succor to my spirit.

"When did we become the same age," I whispered one day to Nonna's photograph, hanging in my hall. "You've smiled at me, benevolent and wise, all of my life. Have I become wise now, too?"

My grandchildren think I am. I have tea and a waiting hankie for their tears and dirt smudges. The monkey broke to pieces years ago in mid-cymbal bash, but he healed many a care before sounding his last clang. My daughters and now granddaughters have grown up with the "just-for-two" tea and sympathy set. When one of them gets it down, life stops for as long as it takes for her to unload her burden. Of all my Nonna's gifts, perhaps that is the most precious: showing me how to comfort and impart love by simply being there and listening . . . no advice necessary.

Now, nearing my seventh decade, holding thoughts of Nonna close at daybreak, I wander through my coffee-scented kitchen, open the back door, stick out my nose, and take a good whiff of fresh morning air. I call to the birds, survey the landscape with black beetle eyes, and plunge my hand into my robe pocket. I pull out an ordinary paisley hankie and bring it to my beak of a nose. Two good honks blast into the silvery dawn.

"*Buon giorno, mia nonna,*" I whisper, "I love you big as the moon and two rainbows."

—*Isabel Bearman Bucher*

What to Name a Grandmother

The stick turned blue," my daughter, Judy, tells me over the phone.

"You're pregnant!" I let out a whoop of joy.

"What do you want to be called?" she asks even before I have a chance to ask her when my first grandchild will arrive.

"What?" I ask.

"Jean-Marc's parents are 'Meme' and 'Pepe,'" Judy says of her husband's parents, who are French and already have three grandsons. "What do you want to be called?"

"Do I have to answer right now?"

"Of course not," she says. "Just think about it."

Well, think, I do. For months and months.

First, I review what I called my grandmothers. "Grandma McEwen" for my paternal grandmother.

No way. Much too formal. My maternal grandmother, Grandma Riber, had been shortened to "Ama" by my older sister, who couldn't say "grandma." Ama was a distinct possibility and definitely in the running. But somehow it just doesn't feel right. I'll think about it.

Judy and her brother, Scott, called their grandmothers "Grammie McEwen" and "Grammie Baker." I like "Grammie," but my grandchildren are definitely not going to have to use my last name. I'll think about it.

Before I know it, seven months pass, the birth is near, and I'm still thinking.

One day Judy and I are sitting on the sofa in her living room, knitting baby bootees—she with blue yarn, I with pink.

"So, have you decided?" she asks.

"Decided what?" I answer, hoping it isn't the question I know is coming.

"What do you want to be called?"

Damn, she hasn't forgotten. I tell her my earlier thoughts, and then say, "How would you feel if I were to be 'Ama'?"

We talk about Ama and the special relationship she and Judy had. The great-grandmother of eight, Ama knew only my son and daughter because three of her other great-grandchildren lived in Arizona and three in Canada. We lived a couple of hours away from Ama, who lived with my mother in New Hampshire. Ama truly enjoyed our visits. When Judy was an infant Ama held her, rocked her, and sang to her tunelessly in German, Danish, or English. As Judy grew older Ama told her stories about her childhood with her eight brothers and sisters in Germany. They took walks together, played games, and made peanut butter cookies from scratch. Ama passed on one month before her 102nd birthday, when Judy was fourteen.

"No," I say, as we both wipe the tears from our eyes, "I can't be Ama."

"There can be only one Ama," Judy agrees with a sniff.

We continue knitting; I continue thinking.

My first thought when I wake up in the morning is, *What do you want to be called?* It's my last thought before I go to sleep. A week before Judy's due date, I start to panic. *Get a grip,* I chide myself. *You haven't been asked to develop a world peace plan. It's just a name.*

Yes, but it's my name. It's a special name, and it has to feel right.

So, do some research, my rational self says. *There must be lots of names for "grandmother."*

I start by asking my friends what their grandchildren call them. I get every answer, from "It doesn't really matter; they'll come up with whatever they want to call you," to "My kids started calling their grandfather 'Cuckoo Head,' and it just stuck."

This is no help.

I go to my small town library. "Do you have any books on what to name a grandmother?" I ask the librarian.

"I've never been asked that before," she says as she consults her computer. "No," she says, "not a one."

This calls for a more up-to-date source. A trip to a bookstore is in order. I find a dozen books on what to name the baby, but not one on what to name the grandma. I don't even bother to ask the clerk.

But I'm a twenty-first-century woman, I decide. This problem requires a twenty-first-century solution.

I turn to the Internet. I Google "names for grandmother" and blow my mind and almost my hard drive with the 875,000 responses from every country in the world. I check out a couple of listings and find lots of choices—*abuela, yaya, baba, mawmaw, bube*, and *nini*, to name a few—but nothing that says "me."

On April 10, I get the call. Judy has given birth to a seven-pound, three-ounce baby boy. As I drive to the hospital, my excitement turns to anxiety. *What do you want to be called? What do you want to be called?* rings through my brain.

I enter Judy's hospital room and am overcome with emotion. Judy radiates the same joy I felt twenty-eight years earlier when I held her for the first time.

"Hi, Mom," Judy whispers. "May I present your grandson, Jean-Phillipe Andre Adourian."

"That's quite a big name for such a little guy," I say.

Judy offers him for me to hold. "You can call him 'J.P.' for short."

Cradling this beautiful child in my arms, I look down on his sweet, sleeping face. "Hello, J.P.," I coo. "I'm your Grandma Glenda, but you can call me 'G.G.' for short."

J.P. opens his eyes and stares at me as if examining my face, and then without a peep, closes them again and returns to his napping.

"G.G.," Judy says. "What a great name! It's so cool. So hip. So fresh."

"So me," I agree. It feels perfect!

"And," Judy adds, "it fits right in with Jean-Marc's French heritage."

"Okay," I say, "G.G. it is."

I hold my grandson closer and softly sing: "A, B, C, D, E, F, G-G..."

J.P. opens his eyes again. Although doctors would disagree, I'm sure I see him smile.

"Look at that," I say, "only five hours old and he already has a sense of humor. Welcome to the family, J.P."

—Glenda Baker

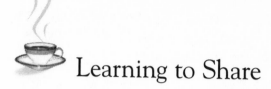

Learning to Share

When I insist we buy the house with an upstairs den, Wife argues, "Honey, I'll never see you again. You just want a cave where you can hibernate like a bear."

Though secretly I admit it might be true, I deny it. Real men don't let little things like guilt stop them from getting the things they deserve—which are:

Computer—where I write undiscovered, un-Pulitzered, non-selling novels. I grudgingly allow Wife the use of it one hour a month to pay the bills.

TV and VCR—which I don't share. It is reserved for old shoot-'em-up westerns and Star Wars reruns.

Rolltop desk—lockable and grandson-proof. Contains my personal fly-tying supplies, complete with feathers from every bird and hair from every animal on the planet, thread of all colors, glue, fine scissors, fish-hooks, etc. Off-limits to everybody. And I only share my flies with the fish who view them with amused skepticism. But I tie them, anyway.

Easy Guy Recliner—complete with reading lamp, shared only with Louis L'amour and Tony Hillerman.

My nirvana has everything a man could need, but sometimes the computer turns moody and sulks in the corner, daring me to write even one worthwhile sentence. Unbidden and untyped by me, guilt-ridden words stream across the screen: How long has it been since you've seen your grandsons?

On TV, John Wayne shoots the bad guys and shouts, "Call your grandsons, Pilgrim!" as he gallops across the plains on the same horse the Indians have shot out from under him a hundred times.

Lately, Easy Guy gives me backaches, and every time I try to read a book, I see pictures of little blue hens and pink roosters: "What does a chicken say?" What does a grandson say? ... "I wanna go see Grandpa!"

And they did.

I am grandsons-sitting while their mother and grandma go to the mall.

My private TV is tuned to the cartoon channel, but no one even glances at it unless I try to change it. Then I hear, "Grandpa, I was watching that!"

My golf clubs, fishing reels, fly-tying vise, feathers, bucktail deer hair, thread, and most of my off-limits worldly possessions lie scattered across the floor.

Homer (the younger) complains, "Grandpa, Hannibal (the older) won't let me play with the magnifying glass!"

"Now, Hannibal," I say. "You must learn to share with your brother." I say it like Charlton Heston thundering commandments from the mountain, though I was an only child and never had to share anything with anyone in my life.

Hannibal applies his five-year-old logic on me. "I don't feel like sharing, Grandpa."

Funny how that always works.

I attempt a compromise. "Okay, Hannibal, be selfish. Homer, play with your computer games."

"I can't, Grandpa! Hannibal already broke it."

"Broke what?"

"The computer."

"He broke my—?" I bite my tongue. "Go watch *Scooby Doo* on TV!"

"I'm tired of *Scooby Doo*."

So am I! "Watch it anyway."

Hannibal opens a drawer and holds up a quart-sized bottle. "Hey, what's this, Grandpa?"

I jerk it away from him. "It's uh—reel oil."

"Boy, you sure must have a lot of rusty reels."

"Just go back to destroying whatever it was you were destroying!"

I put the scotch on a high shelf in the closet and say, "Okay, Homer, sit with me in my Easy Guy, and I'll read you a book."

Homer says, "Hannibal spilled his juice on it; it's all sticky. And he did pee-pee on your chair."

"Did not!" says Hannibal.

"Did too!" says Homer. "Grandpa, I want to play outside."

I see this as a way to get them both out of the house before they completely destroy it. "Okay. Come on, Hannibal, let's go play outside."

"No!" he says. "I want to stay and play in my cave."

"It's my cave!" Homer says. He swings at Hannibal with a three iron. He misses his brother and breaks the reading lamp.

"Knock it off, you two!" I shout. "It's my cave."

"Why?"

"Because I'm bigger'n both of you put together, that's why!" I don't realize I'm yelling.

"What's going on up there?" Mother and Grandma have returned from the mall in the nick of time.

> **Nick of time:** *The measurement of one of the most important nano-moments in human interaction, during which a person's entire universe might possibly be saved from total destruction.*

Nothing bad ever happens during a nick.

I complain to Daughter. "Your kids won't mind me in my own cave, and they're breaking all my stuff."

"Oh, Daddy, you are kidding, aren't you?"

"Yeah," I admit. "We're not perfect, but we're doing okay, aren't we, guys?"

Silence. Daughter looks at me, accusation in her eyes.

I roll my eyes at Grandsons and repeat, "Aren't we, guys?" I wait.

"Ha!" the two little scoundrels finally shout. "Fooled you, Grandpa! You're okay for an old dude."

A heavenly aroma drifts up from the kitchen. Grandma calls, "Who wants brownies?"

"Oh, boy!" I head for the stairway.

"Brownies! Out of the way, Grandpa."

I feel like a runner brushed aside by Hemingway's bulls at Paloma. I collapse on the top step and let the thundering herd pass. "Come back here and clean up this mess!" I plaintively yell with no hope of being heard.

Daughter snickers. "Could it be the boys are getting to be too much for you, old man?"

"Are you kidding? They just happened to get the drop on me that time."

"Well, I just wish you'd stop calling them Hannibal and Homer. I'm afraid they'll forget their real names are Matt and Jacob. And please try to watch your language. You know how they pick up things from you."

"But I don't—"

She glares at me and goes downstairs.

Properly chastised, I lean against the wall and listen to the sounds of Grandma's brownies being devoured.

"Hurry up, Grandpa, or we'll eat them all."

"Be right there, Hannibal."

"When am I gonna get to be Hannibal?" Homer says.

"When I get through being Hannibal."

Homer begins to cry. "I don't want to be Homer anymore. I want to be Hannibal."

Grandma says, "Now Matt, you should learn to share with your brother."

"Okay, Grandma. I'm tired of being Hannibal, anyway."

"Oh, boy!" Homer says. "From now on, everybody calls me Hannibal. What do you want your name to be?" he asks Matt.

The former Hannibal says, "Call me 'Twain.' Some old guy Grandpa knows is named that. He wrote some stories about riverboats and kids. But remember, you're Hannibal and I'm Twain only when we're at Grandpa's house. Everywhere else, I'm Matt and you're Jacob."

Daughter says, "Don't eat the corner pieces, boys. Grandpa always gets them."

"Oh, go ahead," Grandma says. "It's about time the old dude learned to share, too."

The only child rushes down the stairs. "Now, wait a minute!"

—*William M. Barnes*

Jooots and Ohk

I was having another one of those days—when I advanced two steps ahead, only to fall twenty behind. Lately, I seemed to be having more and more of those kinds of days.

The slip-sliding had actually begun a few years earlier, when my pregnant, unmarried daughter came to me in tears.

"Mom, I'm so scared. I don't know how to raise a child by myself."

"I'll help you," I replied. "You are stronger than you realize and will become a wonderful mother. Soon you'll grow to love your baby so much that you'll wonder how you ever lived without her."

Now, here I was, holding to my promise—sometimes by the skin of my teeth. While my daughter worked as an elementary school teacher to support herself and her child, I cared for precious little Alyssa.

My once tranquil and neatly decorated house had been transformed into a virtual romper room. Starting out with such necessary equipment as a rocking chair, infant carrier, baby swing, crib, high-chair, plastic tub, bouncy seat, teddy bears, bottles, pacifiers, bibs, mobiles, stroller, and a carriage, we had progressed to a toddler bed, pink vanity, dolly house (which naturally included at least five hundred tiny pieces of furniture and play people), kitchen sets, a baby doll stroller, and princess everything. That was only on the inside! My car squeezed ever so narrowly into the garage between a sparkly tricycle, a large red wagon, and a Hello Kitty scooter. Formerly a tidy, envious shade of green, my backyard glowed with bright rainbow hues of plastic playhouses, a frog-shaped kiddy pool, a turtle sandbox, and assorted riding toys.

Instead of days filled with adult conversation and lunch with coworkers, my world consisted of *Sesame Street*, Gymboree, Cheerios, and toilet training. Often confused, even discouraged, I worried that the promise I'd made was unattainable. Sometimes I would think, *This isn't fair; I've already raised my children.*

Yet, I loved caring for Alyssa and wouldn't trade one single moment with her for my former job. Her dark brown curls and smile illuminated the room every time she entered. Together we spent many afternoons reading storybooks or walking to a nearby park. Dandelions, squirrels, leaves, and spiders all took on a magical quality through the eyes of Alyssa. It seemed that winter snow was softer, summer afternoons lazier, spring days warmer, and fall leaves brighter when Alyssa was around.

"Damaah, jooots and ohk, pweeze," she would say.

Because all grandmas come equipped with super-heightened deciphering skills, I gladly would get her the orange juice and yogurt she had requested. On a daily basis I could see her growing and changing. When my own three children were young, I was so caught up in the business of everyday living that I wasn't aware of just how fast they were growing.

But this particular day had been extremely trying. Alyssa had already had two potty accidents, spilled milk on the living room carpet, and decorated the coffee table with bright red marker. I was rushing to make an appointment, and she wasn't cooperating at all with getting dressed. From a combination of frustration and menopause, beads of sweat began forming on my forehead. I barely suppressed the temptation to threaten her with the loss of a favorite toy.

As I hurried Alyssa along, secretly wishing it was 4:30 in the afternoon (her mother's arrival time) instead of only 10:30 in the morning, she looked me straight in the eye and said sweetly, "I love you. You're a great damaah."

Then she said it again. "You're a great damaah."

Tears started to trickle down my face. In that moment, I felt like the luckiest woman in the world—because I was.

"Why are your eyes wet, Damaah?" she asked with the simple, beautiful innocence of a young child.

"Sometimes, Alyssa, when grandmas are happy they cry," I said, smiling as I hugged her reassuringly. "And you've made me a very happy grandma."

—Susan J. Siersma

Lord, Love a Duck

Grandma loved ducks, and Grandpa loved Grandma. So every Sunday after church, Grandma, Grandpa, Mom, and the four of us kids crammed into Grandpa's 1968 Datsun Bluebird and headed off to see some ducks.

I'm sure the Bluebird wasn't intended to hold seven people—at least not people as well-fed as our crew. Grandpa insisted on sticking to a complicated seating arrangement. "Otherwise," he said, "we'll break the shock absorbers." Grandma would always add, "Lord, love a duck; we don't want that to happen."

Grandpa had the only driver's license, so he drove each time. My sister, Liz Ann, always got to sit up front. Grandpa said it was because Liz Ann was the smallest; my brothers and I said it was because she was their favorite. I was the oldest, so I sat with Mom in the back, each of us beside a window to balance our weight, and my two brothers were crammed in between Mom and me. Each boy had to prop one foot on the transmission hump.

In summer, it was a miserable arrangement. The Bluebird didn't have air conditioning, and the back windows rolled only halfway down. We'd be glued together with perspiration and road grime; it practically took a shoehorn to pry the four of us out of the back seat. Our clothing was rumpled, our faces were gritty, and Grandma always clucked her tongue at us for getting mussed during the ride. While the rest of us looked like we'd been stuffed inside a Kleenex box, Liz Ann always looked like she'd stepped out of a bandbox.

Grandma chain-smoked Camel nonfilter cigarettes. During cooler weather, when the windows were rolled up, we could hardly see through the windshield for all the smoke. I reckon it wasn't that comfortable a ride in spring or fall, either.

We children got to choose where we wanted to go to see the ducks. If we chose Daniel Boone Park, we fed the domestic ducks that bobbed near the riverbank. In the springtime, ducklings expertly glided behind their mothers on the muddy Kanawha River. At Coonskin Park, the domestic ducks ruled the lake and intimidated other birds that had gotten off-course and made the mistake of stopping for a swim. Sometimes, we'd stop at Coonskin's stables and ride a horse around the corral. Other times, we'd climb around and play on an old train engine that rested on a stranded section of track. If we still had our Sunday clothes on, we weren't allowed to play on the train because we'd get dirty from the coal dust. "Lord, love a duck; we don't want that to happen," Grandma would say, shaking her head.

When we shuffled off to Buffalo (as Grandpa called it when we drove past the little towns of Black Betsy, Red House, and Eleanor to get to the big town of Buffalo), we stopped at a roadside park and fed the greedy wild ducks there. The last time we ever stopped there, I wandered off into the brush and found a big brown dog. He smelled pretty bad, but I petted him anyway. I fed him some leftover stale bread, and he followed me back to the clearing where the picnic table was. I never saw Grandma and Grandpa move as fast as they did that day. Grandpa hollered at me to "Step away from it and get in the car . . . right . . . now." I sadly said goodbye to my doggie friend and ran to the Bluebird. Mom shooed my brothers into the car and scrambled in behind them. Grandma swooped Liz Ann into her arms and jogged to the car. Grandpa opened the Bluebird's trunk and rooted around, looking for his shotgun. It turns out my companion wasn't a dog at all but a bear cub. All of us, baby bear included, escaped unharmed. Grandpa said if the momma bear was around, I'd have been killed. "Lord, love a duck; we don't want that to happen," Grandma said, and we never stopped to picnic at the roadside park again.

Domestic and wild ducks alike scrambled up the banks of the Elk River and waddled across the highway to eat cast-off pieces of hot dog and hamburger buns at the Dairy Queen in Clendenin. The Dairy Queen was situated on a section of land beside Kroger's grocery. Behind the Kroger was an A-frame house. It was the first one I'd ever seen, and I was fascinated by its unique design. One time as I was munching on my hot dog (with chili, slaw, and ketchup) and studying the house, I wasn't paying attention to traffic and nearly got ran over in the Kroger parking lot. After that, we had to sit at the tables and eat so we wouldn't be killed. "Lord, love a duck," Grandma said. "We don't want that to happen."

Sometimes we traveled all the way to Point Pleasant, and Grandma got to enjoy out-of-state ducks on the Ohio River near Tu-Endie-Wei Park. If the museum was open, we'd go inside to see the red hawk Grandpa had donated. He was a fearsome bird, mounted on a perch, with glittering glass eyes; his wings forever outstretched. I always worried he'd come to life and flog me with his awesome spurs. Tu-Endie-Wei was where Chief Cornstalk was killed in 1774. Both my grandparents were of Indian descent, and they mourned each time we visited the Cornstalk monument. There was a five-cent Coke machine at

Tu-Endie-Wei Park. I wasn't strong enough to pull out the bottle, so Grandpa had to help me or I'd lose my nickel every time. Point Pleasant was the only place we traveled to in West Virginia where I could buy a Yoo-Hoo chocolate drink.

Of our diverse duck destinations, my favorite was Zoological Park in Hurricane. I didn't share Grandma's duck fascination, but I did love animals. Zoological Park boasted many types of animals, from tame rabbits and lambs in an open petting section on a rolling hillside, to tigers, bears, and timber wolves that endlessly paced in their cages. The raccoon was one of my favorites. I loved to stick my finger inside the bars. The raccoon hugged my finger with his tiny human-looking hands, and then he'd wash my finger in his water bowl.

On the level section of Zoological Park near the parking area and manager's office was a massive pond with hundreds of domestic ducks. Grandma loved to sit on a park bench beside the pond and feed the ducks stale bread from the red-and-white Purity Maid bags she always brought along on these rides. A chicken wire-encased monkey pen stood high atop a hill. Inside it, dozens of capuchin monkeys swung from poles and chattered at visitors. The pen was about twenty feet by twenty feet, and maybe twelve feet tall, and it sat on a wooden platform with spindly wood legs about three feet off the ground. There was no windbreak, and the afternoon zephyrs ruffled the organ-grinder monkeys' furry sleeves. Grandpa said the manager situated the monkeys on the hill so their stink would blow away from the park. I felt sorry for the little primates. It wasn't like they had a way to bathe.

There was something different in the wind one particular spring Sunday afternoon in Zoological Park. Mom kept my three siblings down by the petting zoo and sent me along with my grandparents. Grandma didn't usually walk the trail due to a heart condition, but this time she said she "felt froggy." When we reached the raccoon pen, I showed her how the raccoon washed my finger. Grandma gave Grandpa a dirty look. "Harold, don't let that child stick her finger in the raccoon cage. They wash their food before they eat it. She could be bitten and get rabies. Lord, love a duck, we don't want that to happen." I sadly bid good-bye to my masked furry friend.

Grandma walked the entire trail that day, and then huffed and puffed her way to the very top of the park—the monkey exhibit. The capuchins put on a show, swinging from pole to pole and jumping up and down. Entranced by their antics, Grandma giggled like a little girl. There was a special glow of pleasure on her face, and Grandpa decided to take a photo to commemorate the occasion. I knew this was a big deal; Grandpa took a photograph only once or twice a year. Grandma and I stood side by side with cheesy grins on our faces, trying to ignore the foul winds blowing toward us while we waited for Grandpa to take his picture. He fumbled with the camera for a couple of minutes, trying to get us in focus. Finally, he told us to move closer to the cage and he'd have his picture. The wind shifted just as Grandma and I backed up. My long hair drifted along with the wind. A single monkey screeched, and suddenly all the capuchins surged forward. I was instantly pinned against the cage as dozens of aggressive monkeys reached through the bars and grabbed at my hair. The brutes jerked my head left and right as each tried to get a better hold. They bashed my skull against the fence wire. It was impossible to break loose from so many grasping monkey claws. Grandma dug her fingernails into my shoulders and tried to yank me free. The monkeys shrieked in protest and pulled on my hair even harder. Grandma yelled. I screamed. The monkeys screeched. Grandma fussed at the monkeys; the monkeys fussed back. Clumps of loose hair floated on the fetid breeze. For a full minute, or so it seemed, Grandpa just stood there, dumbstruck. "Lord, love a duck! Get over here and help us, Harold," Grandma scolded, tugging against the multitude of monkeys who were now tugging against her.

Finally, Grandpa approached the skirmish and opened his pocketknife. I was terrified, wondering what he was going to do. "Hold still. I'm gonna cut you free, honey." He sawed at my hair. Grandpa's pocketknife was razor sharp, but he was no barber. Each time he freed a section of hair, another monkey screamed with delight and jumped away, clutching its prized clump. Grandma was the monkey's adversary, but Grandpa was their accomplice. Shrill angry shrieks shifted to low-pitched excited grunts as Grandpa chopped off my hair, piece by piece. "Just you be patient," Grandpa consoled the monkeys. "It's coming. You'll get yours." After an interminable time, he'd hacked me free. I looked worse than the time I was two years old and cut my hair with Mom's sewing shears.

Grandpa took to laughing so hard, he plopped right down on the ground, tears coursing down his cheeks. Grandma threw him a fierce look, and he stifled his guffaws as he swiped away his tears with an old red handkerchief.

"I swear, Harold, those little heathens remind me of the Indians in the movies, whooping and showing off their scalps." Grandma shook her first ineffectually at the monkeys. The monkeys screeched and gleefully swung from bar to bar, clutching clumps of my hair and defiantly shaking them in the air. They knew they'd won. My head throbbed and my scalp felt like it was on fire. My shoulders burned from Grandma's sharp fingernails. I ran my fingers over the unfamiliar topography of my emergency hair-do. What will the other kids say when I go back to school tomorrow? What could I say had happened?

Grandpa must've read my thoughts. With a twinkle in his warm brown eyes, he said, "You tell them kids at school you fought off fifty monkeys with just a pocketknife, and you won!" I giggled in spite of my discomfort. Grandma said none of it would've happened if she'd stayed down at the duck pond where she belonged. She vowed she'd never walk up the hill again, and she kept her word. Grandpa didn't get his photograph, but he said he'd never forget the image as long as he lived.

From that day on when we went to Zoological Park, I avoided the monkey cage and stayed with Grandma down at the duck pond, because Lord, love a duck, we didn't want that to happen again.

—*Ginger Hamilton Caudill*

"Learning to Share" was first published in the September 2005 premiere issue of *Southern Hum*.

The Froufrou Room

Mom always wanted a proper guest room. She envisioned a suite that whispered of elegance and serenity, not only for her visiting friends and family but also as a retreat for herself. So when my parents decided to remodel their house, instead of launching the project with a more lived-in space, like the kitchen or family room, she convinced Dad to transform the smallest bedroom from a storage room into her dream haven.

The reinvented room would be her escape from dirty dishes, drab furnishings, and the stress of her workweek. Most important, it would be the only room in the house without a television. Only quiet activities—like reading, sleeping, or sewing—would happen in her sanctuary. She might relent and allow a CD player inside, but only soft rock selections could be played.

After much contemplation, Mom chose a delicate, flowery border and a complementary warm shade of pink paint for the walls. My great-grandmother's Victorian dresser and a gold-rimmed mirror claimed prominent spaces on opposite walls. For this special space, comfort and style ruled over practicality and frugality, and Mom chose a luxurious down duvet to cover the new, but too soft, full-sized bed. Dad grumbled about the amount of time, effort, and cash being expended on the "froufrou room," as he dubbed it. Still, I caught him smiling a few times at Mom's enthusiasm.

My grandmother received the honor of the first visit. Mom ate up my grandmother's compliments, taking special pride in her praise of the homemade potpourri of dried apples and cinnamon sticks.

After the trial run, Mom declared the room ready and proceeded to escape there as many times as she could. I'm sure she didn't get away as much as she wanted to, but she found a weekly time slot while Dad watched football games. I often searched the house on Sunday afternoons to find Mom unwinding in her bentwood rocker with a magazine and cup of tea in the froufrou room. She told me she was pleased with each intricate selection in the room, from the French country needlepoint bench to several lace doilies. It fit her dreams perfectly.

Then Mom became Grammy and added a bassinet and visiting granddaughter to the room. Both baby and bassinet coordinated well with the elegant theme. Angelic soft curls and frilly layers of lace added an air of youth and humanity to the room's ambiance. The lights seemed to shine brighter on all the beloved furnishings and knickknacks.

Instead of having calm reflection and quiet activity, Mom now found herself tickling tiny feet and bouncing the sweet bundle on her knees. The new grandmother's face lit up with each giggle and coo. Where once she had sought relaxation she now found rejuvenation.

Before long, diapers and spare onesies snuck into an empty drawer in the dresser. Picture books tiptoed into a basket underneath the nightstand, and toys crept onto the floor of the closet. A cursory glance of the room showed an adult sanctuary, but children had most definitely invaded.

When the delicate little angel began to walk, the room changed even more. Mom never cringed or sighed, but quietly made necessary adjustments to her haven. Antique plates were elevated. The fragile, refinished bench was off-limits to everyone except a family of porcelain dolls. The granddaughter added some of her own touches, too, like the barnyard animals who claimed a prominent spot beside the crystal perfume atomizers on the bureau.

By the time the little princess received a baby brother, the froufrou room no longer whispered "refinement." It shouted "grandkids!" A waterproof mattress pad and a rainbow sleeping bag replaced the hand-embroidered comforter and two-hundred-count Egyptian cotton sheets. Red and purple markings from permanent markers adorned one corner of the wall. A plastic block castle commandeered the sewing machine's former position. And despite Mom's earlier television boycott, a new TV/DVD combination dominated the dresser top, sitting upon a lovely doily.

After running a few errands the other day, I walked into my parents' home. Most of the house was quiet and still. Coming from the froufrou room, I heard the strains of "Old MacDonald" with crashes of a cymbal added for emphasis.

I opened the door and saw my mom sitting on the hard floor, her back hunched over and my two children climbing over her, vying for more lap space. *Poor Mom*, I thought. All she ever wanted was a fancy room of her own, separate from the rest of the world, where she could curl up in a rocking chair or settle into the comfy bed to rest or read. For a few measly months, she had had her dream. Then I went and ruined it for her by invading her special place with grandkids. Now that I'm a mother myself, I realize why Mom wanted a space of her own. Sometimes, the demands of a young family wear me to the bone. I can only imagine how thirty more years of this might tire someone out.

"Oh, Mom, you really wanted this to be a beautiful guest room. And look at what my two rascals have made of it. And of you."

My mother—with her glittery cheeks, hot-pink lipstick, a dress-up shawl around her shoulders, and cookie crumbs on her lap—sat amid plastic teacups, blocks, flash cards, and modeling clay remnants. She hugged my little princess and prince to her chest.

"This is precisely the sort of guests I have always dreamed of entertaining," she said.

I glanced around the room at the ornamental treasures and the children's messy excess, and saw that the two actually mixed quite well into a perfect décor of elegance and ebullience. Then I looked at Mom, sitting there contentedly in her fancy childish getup, and I saw the truth reflected in her brightly shining eyes. Her glowing face said that the love and joy she'd gained from her grandchildren more than made up for the small sacrifices she'd made in altering a sophisticated room, which had, in reality, been made all the more lovely by these precious additions. Mom smiled. I smiled back and then joined them on the most elegant, grape-juice-stained carpet I've ever seen.

—*Jodi Gastaldo*

Tender Hearts

I had just stepped into the doorway of my son's bedroom when I caught a ball-like flurry of arms and legs bouncing down the stairs, identifiable by the sparkle of shiny bifocals and a hint of salt and pepper curls flashing past. My mother, taking a sudden shortcut.

She rolled to a stop amid scattered plates and unfinished bread crusts, having lost her hold on the trays she was carrying. Mother had just retrieved the lunch dishes from the children's indoor picnic we'd spread out on the upper level of Chris's room. But the four steps down gave her trouble and she tripped, performing several reluctant somersaults. Now she lay on the carpet, wounded, massaging her foot and attempting a brave face.

My hand flew to my mouth, suppressing a gasp. My poor little mother! That must have really hurt. As much as I wanted to be compassionate, I could feel that old familiar desire to chuckle tickling my over-abundant funny bones. A lover of slapstick comedy, I saw humor in every pratfall and pitfall, even when it wasn't meant to be comic relief. I mean, I really did love Lucy. But I couldn't laugh at this, at my sweet mother's mishap. I placed the other hand over my mouth to lock in my amusement. *Don't laugh. Don't laugh.* A giggle escaped and then another. Soon I was clasping my sides, shrieking with laughter, even emitting an occasional snort, until tears were flowing down my face.

My mother looked at me with what appeared to be dazed disbelief and then, probably against her will, the corners of her mouth began to curve upward until she joined in with a giggle or two of her own. Tears were also filling her eyes, but I was sure they were not the joyful kind.

"You and your weird sense of humor," she said, snickering in spite of herself. She continued to rub her foot and groaned a little. "I suppose I did look silly. Still, imagine laughing at someone who just fell down the stairs." She shook her head.

Mother was right. What kind of a daughter was I? But before I had a chance to morph into Florence Nightingale mode, my ten-year-old son, Chris, leapt from the upper level, across all four steps, and landed next to Mother—a superhero without the cape. He knelt down, and touching her foot with a gentle hand, asked, "Grandma, are you okay?"

Mother melted under his tender approach, the empathy causing her tears to flow without restraint.

I, of course, wondered where this boy of mine had gained such a sensitive nature. If I looked in the mirror, I wouldn't find the role model there. Maybe it was a gift from his grandma; her kindness was legendary.

"I'll be all right," she said between little sobs. "I just need to sit awhile."

But she wasn't all right. Mother's ankle quickly swelled beyond her shoe size and began to turn the colors of a vivid sunset, deep yellow and purple. She couldn't walk unassisted, so Dad and I supported her on each side as she limped into the living room and collapsed into a comfy chair. Chris placed a pillow under her foot, now elevated on our ottoman, and patted his grandma's hand.

We served her tea and an ice pack. Chris brought her magazines and adjusted her pillow support; he didn't leave her side. After Mother had downed a dose of aspirin, the family helped her to the car so Daddy could drive her to their home more than two hours away.

"I'm fine. It just hurts a little now," Mother said. She gave us farewell kisses before my father deposited her into the back of their big Chevrolet, one leg stretched across the leather seat, the offending foot propped on a pillow Chris had brought from the house. "I'll keep you posted."

"Grandma, stay off your foot, okay?" Chris lingered at her door. "I'll call you."

Monday came and went with no word from Mother. Chris began to pester me on Tuesday.

"Can we call Grandma today?" he asked.

"She said she'd call. She'll call in her own time." That seemed clear and reasonable to me. In a time before cordless telephones were popular, why make her hobble across a room if she was resting?

By Thursday, I, too, was beginning to wonder what had happened and gave in. When she answered, it was a relief to hear her voice. Soon we were chatting, our voices animated as we discussed our news. I was just sharing why I didn't like my new perm when Chris appeared, his expression earnest and pleading, indicating that he would like to talk to his grandma. I handed him the phone, cautioning him that Mother and I were not finished visiting. "Don't hang up," I said.

He cupped the receiver between tanned hands and plopped on a ladder-back chair in the dining room, one leg swinging back and forth.

"Hi, Grandma," he said. "How is your foot?"

Rats. I had forgotten all about her fall the minute we'd started chatting. Mother turned the conversation away from herself, as always, to what interested her children. I felt a rush of shame wash over me as I realized that what had interested me most was mostly me.

Chris gave me a rundown of the doctor's report, placing his hand over the receiver to relay the information, his voice husky with emotion. Grandma had pulled some ligaments and fractured the bones in the bottom of her foot. Her leg was purple clear to the knee! The doctor was upset because she waited so long to make an appointment. She would be on crutches for weeks.

And I hadn't even bothered to ask.

I looked in wonder at my young son, who is so much like his gentle grandma. I said a silent prayer of thanks and tried to imagine what kind of man he might become. *Would he be a great man of compassion, changing the world with one kindness at a time?*

For now, I would settle for a change in myself. A big change, initiated by the example of a ten-year-old boy with a tender heart.

—Cathy Elliott

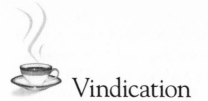 Vindication

I have yet to meet a mother who, at some point, has not questioned her mothering skills and sanity. I am no exception. Why I've never wondered how I would rate as a grandmother, I can't tell you. But now that I am a grandmother, one thing I do know is that my grandchildren's role is to open my daughter's eyes to the fact and to show me that I wasn't such a bad mother after all.

Grandmotherhood has given me a reward that is worth all the rolled eyes, exasperated sighs, slammed doors, and "you don't understands" that I got from my children: vindication. I've seen it and heard it for myself, and I am tickled pink to tell you that all those quirky things I came up with in my moments of sheer desperation as a parent are alive and well and living in my daughter's house.

Cases in point …

During one of my visits to my daughter's home, she needed to run some errands and I tagged along. With my grandson properly tucked into his car seat in the back seat, we headed out. It wasn't long before he started fussing, with the occasional howl and screech thrown in for good measure. After trying unsuccessfully to calm or at least distract him by passing him a bottle, crackers, books, and toys, not to mention singing a song and blasting the radio, I heard the words come out of my daughter's mouth that were music to my ears.

"Look! Look! A monkey! There, in the tree! It's a monkey! Do you see him? Look! Look! There's another one. Oh, look! Another one!"

There was quiet from the back seat for the next ten minutes as my grandson scanned the streets for monkeys. As a child, my daughter had searched for every animal imaginable. I even had her friends doing it.

Since the time she uttered her first words, my daughter has always been a "talker." And it wasn't just a stage with her; it is a lifelong condition. As a new mother, she would drone on and on to her first child, carefully articulating what the child was or was not to do and painstakingly explaining the whys and wherefores. I'd stand off to the side, rolling my eyes and biting my tongue, and the kid would just stare at her with glazed eyes. She kept this up for years, until about the time the second child was ready for kindergarten. Then, suddenly, she began to speak like me, in short, to-the-point sentences, which she followed up with "consequences" that looked more than vaguely familiar. "Mommy, I'm thirsty," was met with, "Well, go get a drink." Two squabbling children got a two-word command—"Stop that!—followed by a time-out on the magazine rack in the bathroom.

I'm an animal lover, a passion I've happily passed along to my children. As they were growing up, together we nursed baby birds and orphaned squirrels and housed a menagerie of pets, from dogs and cats, to fish, hamsters, birds, and even a snake. Snakes were the one animal my daughter didn't take to, and she was not at all pleased when her brother was allowed to keep a ball python in the house, especially since we had to feed him "cute" little mice. Twice the snake escaped its container and slithered to a hiding place somewhere in the house. Naturally, it was my daughter who found him, quite by accident and accompanied by piercing screams—the first time in her closet, the second in the bathtub. When Tom the Snake finally met his demise, she informed us that she would never, under any circumstances, have a snake in her house.

My grandson is almost three. When he wants something, he stays very focused on it for an exceed- ingly long time. He is, shall we say, bull-headed. It is a trait he comes by naturally and that I know all too well, having been the "mean old mom" who tangled for years with a certain iron-willed little girl who is now his mother. Not long ago, my daughter and I took the children to a pet store, just for fun. It turned out to be anything but. The little guy didn't care a bit about dogs or cats, fish or birds, or even turtles and cute little mice. Yep, that's right. The thing he zeroed in on, the creature he wanted with every fiber of his mighty little being, was a snake . . . a big snake . . . a massive yellow snake. Daughter said no. Grandson had a meltdown. Grandma left the store, barely suppressing a snicker. Even outside, I could hear his screams. A few minutes later, out came Mom, lugging a wailing, flailing toddler. The expression on her face—a contorted mix of horror, humiliation, frustration, and steely grit—was priceless. *It's not easy being mean, is it?*

On one particularly trying day with my young ones, I attempted to steal a few moments of peace and solitude in the only place available for desperate mothers—the bathroom. I had barely taken a deep breath when there came a knocking on the door. I did the only thing I could. I didn't answer. The knocking started again, this time accompanied by the occasional plaintive "Mama?" This continued for a few more minutes until I heard myself say, "She isn't here." Silence. I could almost hear the wheels turning in her head. Then a small voice said, "Who are you?" I pretended to be a very nice person named Suzy, and we chatted for a few moments until my daughter was satisfied it wasn't me and went away.

Last week I picked up the ringing phone to hear her grown-up voice call out in that same plaintive tone: "Mama?" In the background I could hear some tapping on the door. "Mom, help. I'm in the bathroom. . . ." I'm still smiling.

To my grandchildren: Thank you. Thank you for being just enough like your Mom that you can irritate her as much as she did me. Thank you for letting me enjoy seeing little minds and bodies grow by leaps and bounds without having to feel responsible for the outcome. Thank you for the drawings and the crumpled cookie you stuck in my suitcase. Thank you for showing my cat that he is not the king of the world. By the way, the vet says he'll recover from his nervous breakdown by the time you visit again. Last but not least, thank you for loving your mom as much as I do.

—May Mavrogenis

Me, a Grandmother? No Way!

I have always had an independent and adventurous spirit. Though my husband and I have much in common, we also have certain interests that we don't share—and that works well for both of us. Early on in our marriage, Gil and I agreed to have children while we were young, in part to allow ample time after we'd raised our family to spend with each other, traveling and enjoying our shared interests, as well as to pursue our individual hobbies.

Neither my sons nor my husband share my love of horses and camping, and so during the family years, I didn't ride or camp as often as I might have liked. As the two boys grew into men and independence, I rode and camped alone. I soon came to love the freedom, lack of responsibilities, and solitude—just Dantu, my loyal pinto horse, and me. At the age of forty, I enjoyed my first adventure vacation, sleeping in a tipi and riding snowcapped mountains in Montana and Wyoming in pursuit of cattle. No empty-nest syndrome for this mother of two grown sons; my heart's desires would take several lifetimes to experience.

Likewise, I had little interest in being a grand-parent. The boys agreed that neither I nor their father were ideal "grandparent material." And forget the possibility of their future children spending a summer's vacation or even a weekend at Grandma and Grandpa's house, with "Dad off hunting in another state" and "Mom being no-telling-where with a horse." Sometimes my sons talked about someday having kids, and I would remind them that there were "no built-in babysitters in this family" and they'd have to raise their kids themselves, just as we had.

Then one day Leah, our oldest son's girlfriend, sat at our kitchen counter and talked with me about wanting children and her "ticking clock." At twenty-five, she'd decided to have a child but maybe not marriage—and our son was the father. I had no clue of the impact her decision would have on our lives.

Soon, Gil and I were looking over ultrasounds of the baby and discussing my worries that our "should-be daughter-in-law," Leah, and our son might part. And where would that place us in the scheme of a grandchild's life? I couldn't come to love a child only to have him or her snatched away by a stepfather.

Leah consistently assured us that she wanted her baby
to have as much love as possible, and that meant the
baby would always be part of our lives, regardless of
whom she lived with or eventually married. Her child
would be our grandchild—forever and always.

When Miranda Jean was born, at 5:00 A.M. on
April 4, 1996, I was on my way to a mule-riding
adventure down the Grand Canyon. Leah promised
a birth before I left, and she fulfilled that promise.
I boarded a plane at 6:00 A.M. knowing a healthy
granddaughter had been born but nothing more. I
was happy and excited about the news and looking
forward to getting to know my new grandchild . . .
later. But I had no desire to cancel my plans, and no
designs on transforming into a doting grandmother.

At the canyon I met a grandmother accompanied
by her daughter and three granddaughters, all on
mules. She told me she was fulfilling her promise to
ride with them into the canyon when the youngest
turned sixteen. I had forgotten about all the times
when I'd been alone and watched families camping
and riding together. Then, the love of my hobby had
been enough and all that mattered. Suddenly, I realized what being a grandmother meant: I might have
someone, another female, my own granddaughter, to
do these things with me.

I went scurrying to a gift shop, and I mailed
Miranda Jean her first invitation into my life. It was

a postcard of an Indian mother toting her child in a papoose. On the back, I wrote a note to Miranda, saying that she didn't know me yet, but the day would come when we would ride mules down into the Grand Canyon together. Ten years later, that card is in Miranda's cedar chest, along with dozens of other mementos of the many wonderful experiences we've had together.

Horses and camping are two of Miranda's favorite things. Of course, she is also a chatterbox. More than once I've shushed her as we ride through the woods: "This is supposed to be a peaceful nature trail, Miranda Jean! You've scared away every animal within a five-mile radius." Our most heated disagreement occurred in the woods. She didn't want to return to camp, and it was dusk. How I love that about her!

The fun and adventures that Miranda and I have shared are second only to the love and affection between us . . . which is right up there with the special bond between my granddaughter and my husband. When she was a toddler, I remember her running down the driveway with arms outstretched and yelling, "Papaw Gil, Papaw Gil!" Tears welled in Gil's eyes as he scooped her in his arms. She affects him the same way today.

Miranda's maternal grandmother died suddenly from heart failure when Miranda was two, and our should-be daughter-in-law Leah stressed, even more, how important we are in Miranda's life. When Miranda visits or sleeps over, we sometimes bake a pie to take to Papaw Ron. She reminds me that Papaw Ron doesn't have anyone to bake him pies anymore, so she must do it.

Leah needn't have reminded us of the importance of our roles as Miranda's grandparents. Though it was good to hear, we wouldn't have it any other way. Miranda fills our souls with sweet, smoky excitement, as vivid as her dancing hazel eyes speckled with gray flecks. She inspires me to sing and dance and run and tumble in leaves. Even now, in the fall, we rake leaves into a huge pile near the chicken pen. We run up and then down the hill and then flop atop the pile, hooting and hollering. We build snowmen at midnight. We pick blackberries and cherries and make jelly in the summer. When a special event takes place at school, she calls Gran'ma and Papaw Gil. And our famous conglomeration of a monster cookie recipe is featured in her school's cookbook.

Miranda doesn't do slumber parties; she does "sleepovers." During one at our house when she was three, I went into my bedroom to comb out my long, wet hair. Sitting at the vanity, resembling Cousin It, I was attempting to detangle the mess. Unbeknownst to me, Miranda entered the room and stood quietly watching. Suddenly a small hand rested on my leg, and a sweet voice whispered, "Gran'ma, is that the side you talk out of?" With both hands, I yanked a makeshift part and yelled, "Yes!" We laughed until we cried.

I used to read to Miranda at bedtime; now she reads to me. I used to write her poems; now she's the poet. Our list of trade-offs magically grows.

Miranda helps with everything. Unlike those two sons of mine, she is eager to plant flowers and to pick up baby chicks at the post office, a ritual we began when she was two. She's been gathering eggs since before she was walking. She's a real chicken guru—and a city girl to boot.

One of the things I love most about Miranda (and a trait she shares with yours truly) is her iron will. Of course, that means we sometimes go head to head. One of our numerous disagreements ensued over fishing. She wanted to fish, but she didn't want to put the wiggly night crawlers on the hook. When I insisted that if she wanted to be an angler she had do it all, she threaded the lively worm onto the hook, though not without a fair amount of fuss and "yucks." The channel catfish she caught was bigger than her Snoopy rod. It took both of us—while yelling victory at the top of our lungs—to lug it to the house for Papaw Gil to photograph.

Miranda is an animal and plant lover, another trait we share. She prefers cats to breathing, and we disagree over the number of cats any one barn can house. She's finally come to terms with the fact that Gran'ma and Papaw Gil can afford to neuter or spay only so many kitties.

Miranda was with me when it was time to let go of our thirty-five-year-old, blind and deaf donkey. I worried that seeing an animal euthanized might be too traumatic for her, but Leah assured that Miranda insisted on being there. She wanted to say goodbye to Sally, and she didn't want Gran'ma to be alone. We groomed and loved Sally before the vet arrived, and only once, after Sally took her last breath, did Miranda walk away to discreetly wipe her eyes. In those moments, at six years of age, she shouldered a maturity and understanding of death that I've seen in few adults.

Miranda is always plotting something new. Her latest brainstorm came just the other day. "We have to write a book," she said excitedly. "I want to call it *Miranda Jean's Crazy Gran'ma*." I am already partial to the title.

From my childhood, there was a deep red rose with a fragrance that haunted me. I wanted to find it, to know its name and plant one in our flower garden. Gil had grown accustomed to me walking the rows of roses at garden centers and public gardens, sniffing. After decades of sniffing hundreds of thousands of roses, I'd never found one even similar to the fragrance of my memories.

When Miranda was a year old, I was doing the sniffing ritual at a plant display at Kmart and stopped abruptly in my tracks. Gil saw the look on my face and that I was fighting back tears, and hurried to see what was wrong. At first, I just held out the label, unable to speak. Finally, I showed him the name on the tag. I had found my rose, and it is named "Mirandee." I later learned that Mirandee is a hybrid of the rose "Miranda," which is the actual rose of my childhood. No wonder that rose had been so special to me. Perhaps it foretold the unique beauty and wonder of my granddaughter.

Our Miranda blooms gloriously with every season. She fills our lives with color, sweetness, spice, and joy. I wouldn't trade being Miranda's Gran'ma for all the "independence" in the world. It is the most magnificent adventure of my life.

—*Jo Ann Holbrook*

Not for a Very Long Time

"Nana, how old are you?" Jason, my six-year-old grandson, asked, peering up at me as we walked hand in hand toward the ice cream shop.

"Fifty-six," I answered without hesitation.

His slate blue eyes widened a bit as a warm breeze ruffled his auburn hair. He sure is one of ours, I thought. With that dust of Ireland sprinkled across his brow in the same pattern of freckles I see in the mirror every morning, I'd have no problem claiming him if he should wander off.

"Wow. How did you get to be that old?" he said with something akin to awe in his voice.

"I don't know," I answered truthfully. "I was young for a long, long time, and then one day I was in the supermarket and some kid behind the counter called me 'ma'am,' and that was it."

"Did he make you old?"

"Nah," I laughed. "In fact, I'm not sure I'm old yet. I think he just got confused for a minute."

"How old do you have to be to be old?"

"I'll let you know when I get there, but it won't be for quite a while. As long as I can keep up with you, we'll know it hasn't happened yet," I said as we entered the shop. "So, what's it gonna be, kiddo? Hot fudge sundae or banana split?"

"Both," he dared, testing to see how far Nana would let him go.

"Both, it is," I agreed.

"Really?"

"Sure, why not? We'll get one of each and share. That way we can have everything we want and stuff ourselves silly."

Anyone who really knows me is aware I love ice cream and will use any excuse in the world to get some, even going so far as using an unsuspecting grandson as an accomplice.

"What are we gonna do today?" he asked the next morning. We were both wearing our Sponge Bob pajamas and eating Fruit Loops in front of the TV.

"I'm glad you asked," I said, pulling a large box out from under the coffee table.

"Rollerblades!" he screeched. "Oh man, I've been waiting my whole life for Rollarblades. My Mom always says, 'No, you're too young.'"

"Too young, too old, we don't believe in that around here," I assured him. "Finish your cereal and let's get going."

"I didn't know you could skate," Jason commented as we sat side by side strapping on our blades at the park.

"Who do you think taught your Mom? Watch this," I said as I took off.

I circled the track at a fair pace and finished with a backward flourish right in front of him.

"Get a move on, boy," I urged. "We're burning daylight."

It didn't take long for him to get the hang of his new skates, and soon he was looping around the track with the best of them. After skating, we spent the afternoon at the movies, covertly pelting the kids around us with popcorn and ducking their counter-assaults as best we could.

Later, after hearing his prayers and tucking him into bed, I eased my sore muscles with a soak in the Jacuzzi and a glass of my favorite merlot. *You should take it easy*, I thought. *You're not as young as you used to be. Act your age.* Then, on second thought, I reasoned that part of my reward for having raised my own four children was getting to be a kid all over again with my grandchildren. *Stuff it*, my inner child ordered my inner granny. *I'm not nearly as old as I plan to be, so get out of my way. I've got some horseback riding to do tomorrow.*

Okay, I admit it. The saddle was hard and my equestrian skills were rusty, but I was able to keep up the next day. We took a two-hour ride through the trees and meadows of a local farm where they rent horses by the hour, stopping midday for a picnic lunch in the shade of a tree that probably witnessed more than a few Civil War battles. I imagined the ghosts of young soldiers nodding in approval at the sight of children and families sharing a meal on the ground they'd given their lives to defend. A mix of old and new, history and promise, seemed to come together for a moment in time.

"Time to saddle up," our guide announced. "Need any help getting back on your horse, ma'am?" he asked.

Before I had a chance to respond with a polite "No, thank you," Jason answered on my behalf.

"She can do it all by herself. She's Nana, and she can skate and eat two kinds of ice cream at once, and she can still keep up with me. She's not old yet. When she is, then you can call her 'ma'am.' But that won't be for a very long time—right, Nana?"

"Right, Jason," I said, relishing the amused expressions on everyone's faces. "That won't be for a very long time."

—*Bobbi Carducci*

 Life Cycles

It took fifteen years for me to realize that my son's death had killed me, too. I ate dead, slept dead, worked dead, made love to my husband dead. And when going through the motions of loving him became too painful to bear, I divorced him dead. But had you asked me at any point during those fifteen years if I were alive, I would have told you yes. My two daughters and all of my friends would have vouched for me.

I am standing at the bedside of my daughter Susan in a birthing room in Yale–New Haven Hospital. I am here at her invitation, watching in amazement at how differently birthing is done these days. Forty years ago, when my son was born, I was strapped on a metal table in a freezing cold delivery room with bright lights blazing down. Susan has spent the night in a cozy warm bed in a dimly lit room, with soft music playing, a gentle midwife in attendance, and her husband at her bedside holding her hand.

The birth is near. The midwife invites me to come and stand behind her at the foot of the bed. She says the baby has crowned. She wants me to see. I move to the foot of the bed and stand, a little behind the midwife, off to the side, and I see. But the glimpse of a child about to be born spins me backwards in time to a different delivery room, a different baby, and the images overlap in my mind.

I am nineteen years old, lying on a metal table in the Naval Hospital in Philadelphia. My husband, a petty officer assigned to the Philadelphia base, is not allowed in the room. In those days, giving birth was still considered the exclusive domain of women, nurses, and doctors. My legs are elevated and wrapped in canvas leggings; my feet are fastened in metal stirrups. Vomit has trickled from my mouth, run down my chin, and settled in a sour puddle in the hollow of my neck. No one makes a move to wipe it away, and I cannot wipe it because my wrists are strapped to the table.

I am stunned by the pain of this rite of passage into the woman's world of my mother and grand-mothers. It arches my back, splits my body. A scream that I recognize as mine echoes off the walls of the room, lingers in the air for an eternity, then loses the breath that expelled it and drifts away. The scream fades into another dimension and is replaced by a squeaky little cry that seems to be coming from the direction of my feet. I follow the sound, and there, held upside down above my thighs, I see a tiny wrinkled creature with skin the color of stone. The tiny creature's cries grow stronger; and with each new cry, color flows through its body, turning the stone-gray skin to pink. The color spreads steadily, warm and vibrant pink, from his feet to his wrinkled legs, across his belly, where the thick blue cord still connects his body to mine, into his arms and hands, down to his outraged little face, all screwed up and squalling, and down to the top of his head.

Twenty-five years later, I sat at the deathbed of the beautiful and beloved grownup the tiny wrinkled baby had become. I held his hand, stroked his brow, and watched in silence as the miracle of birth reversed itself right before my eyes. Watched as the skin that once had turned from gray to pink turned back again to stone-gray. Watched as the cancer against which he'd fought so bravely for four long, wearying years defeated him after all.

My daughter's grunts are primitive, filled with desperate pain. The midwife is bent beside me, pressing Susan's thighs, urging her to "Push! ... Push! ... Push!" The movements and sounds around me mingle with memory. The air crackles with the otherworldly current I recall from the night of my son's death. And though it makes no sound, it seems to say, as it did that other night: *Pay attention. . . . Pay close attention. . . . Something sacred is about to happen here.*

I do not want to pay attention. I do not want to be here. I do not want to witness my daughter's pain or relive my own. I want to hide my face, to scream, to run. But a force stronger than I, stronger than any power I have ever known, holds me there.

In a movement so deft and swift I was astonished to realize that it had happened at all, the midwife pulled my daughter's baby from her body and placed it on her belly.

"You have a son," she said.

Her announcement is soon mingled with the sound of a squeaky little cry. It is a cry from my daughter's son, a cry from my son, a cry from a deathbed, a cry from my heart. Tears slip down my face as something that has long encased me—something hard and unyielding as armor—begins to crack and fall away.

At Susan's beckoning, I move to her bedside and watch as the once-stone-colored baby nestled in her arms turns rosier and rosier with each new breath he takes. My tiny grandson is pink and whole and healthy and alive. And so, at last, am I.

—*Virginia Rudd*

Grandma Will Save Me

When I was a little boy, visiting Grandma was a real treat. My grandparents lived in a little white bungalow bordering the rural area on the western edge of Spencer, Iowa. A white rail fence surrounded the front yard, and that fence served as my horse when I became Roy Rogers or the Lone Ranger.

Grandma usually wore a smile for me, with or without her false teeth. Her quick wit and infectious laugh made helping her with chores a joy rather than a burden. Only once did I see her lose her sense of humor, on a day that started out like any other normal visit to Grandma's house.

At mid-morning of that day, as I was playing with an assortment of bugs in the window well, Grandma came running around the house from the front yard with her big apron flapping. When I looked up, I did not see her usual round happy face; instead, I caught a glimpse of a wild look in her dark eyes. Wordlessly, she grabbed me by one of my arms, hoisted me up away from the basement window, plunked me by her side, and hustled me toward the back door. As I tried to ask what kind of game we were playing, all I got was a threatening glare and "Shush!" as she tightened her grip on my skinny arm. My confusion grew as we flew past the back door. This commotion was totally unlike my grandma, and as much as I wanted to know what was going on, I knew better than to ask dumb questions at that time. In a flash, we rounded the back of the house. Grandma stopped and took off her dusty gardening shoes. Gasping for breath, she managed to whisper that I was not to make a peep, and I was glad I had decided to keep quiet.

In her stocking feet, she quickly dragged me to the back door and gingerly opened the outer screen door. She held me close at her side as we entered the landing. She paused and turned around to crane her neck and peer through the screen. She gave a quick glance to the front of the house, and then she eased the screen door closed so that it would not slam and carefully shut the back door and locked it. I gaped at the beads of sweat streaming down the side of her reddened face. By this time, her tension had started to frighten me. What exactly my grandmother had witnessed was known only to her. I guessed she didn't want to frighten me by telling me what kind of horrible creature she had seen. I imagined any number of monsters that could be on the loose and roaming the streets of Spencer in the late spring afternoon.

We leaped the two stairs from the landing and up into the kitchen, and Grandma cautiously closed and locked a second door behind us. I figured that whatever was out there certainly would not get past those sturdy locked doors. Then I remembered the fearsome giant rabbit that my mom had tried to pass off as the Easter bunny. Someone once told me that rabbits had very sharp teeth. I began to worry whether such a giant rabbit could gnaw through solid wood doors. As I thought about this more, I realized that there was also the boogey-man to consider. I knew he was alive and well, always lurking in the shadows, ready to snatch little kids. But did he come out in the daytime? More important, I wondered whether it was true that he could walk through solid walls. I hoped that Grandma would be able to protect me from the ferocious monster that was terrorizing her neighborhood.

As we rushed through the kitchen and the sitting room, I looked up at Grandma for reassurance. I thought I detected fear in her eyes; that did not reassure me. I started to suggest that we might be safer in her root cellar, but she put a finger up to her lips and reminded me to be quiet. Before we entered the solarium, located at the front of her house, she stopped trying to catch her breath and squatted down to look me in the eyes. She spoke in a serious tone, and I'll bet that if I could have looked in a mirror at that moment, I would have seen my hair standing straight up on end.

"I need you to be very quiet, Scooter," she said. "You can't make a sound; don't even breathe until I tell you. Just do exactly as I tell you."

By that time I was so scared, I felt my only hope was to trust Grandma. That way, I figured, Grandma would protect me from whatever was coming for me. With wide eyes, I nodded obediently.

"Get down on your hands and knees," she commanded.

"Okay," I squeaked.

I wondered whether I might get eaten by a monster yet, but I followed Grandma's example as she got down on her hands and knees and crawled into the solarium. As I crawled into the room behind her, the sun was filtering through the narrow slits of the drawn blinds. The doorbell rang, and I froze. Through the blinds I could make out the shadow of a humanlike form. The boogey-man? My grandma carefully laid her large round body upon the braided rug covering the freshly waxed wooden floor. I heard her wheezing, and I felt my heart pounding. The bell rang again, and I twitched as it startled me. I closed my eyes, hoping that he didn't have the power to walk through solid walls.

For what seemed like a horribly long time, we lay there, Grandma and me, filled with fear and dread. I had heard that if you pretended to be dead, wild animals would leave you alone and not eat you. Unfortunately, I was not so sure that would work with the clever boogey-man. Finally, the shadow moved away from the front door. I looked at Grandma, who was intently following the retreating shape with her eyes. When it disappeared, she got to her knees and crawled over to the blinds, opened a small slit in the blinds and peered out.

"He's leaving," Grandma said, still whispering.

My fear melted when I noticed that the tension in her face had been replaced by a triumphant grin. We'd done it! We had pretended we were dead, and it had worked. Maybe it wasn't the boogey-man. Maybe it was some kind of wild animal. Maybe it was some kind of monster that only adults knew about. Just to be sure, I asked Grandma.

"What kind of creature was that Grandma?"

"Oh, that was one of those pesky Fuller Brush salesmen," she said in a disdainful manner. "You did real good, Scooter!" So saying, she smothered me in her big arms with a victorious hug.

As she held me, I realized that Grandma had saved me and she had just given me my first lesson on how to outsmart such fearful creatures.

—Dennis Jamison

An American Babushka

The squalls of a baby pierce the Saturday afternoon meditative calm of St. Vladimir's Russian Orthodox Church. Our infant grandson is lifted, naked and squirming, from his third immersion in the ornate silver font and elevated to God in the arms of the priest. Seven-week-old Sasha's eyes and fists are tightly closed; bursts of fury expand his tiny chest.

The priest returns him to Galina, his Russian babushka, grandmother, and she and Iulia, his mother, murmur soothingly as they dry and diaper him. Galina carries him to one side of the church and then the other, holding him high to the icons resting side by side on wooden ledges. He's stopped crying and just looks puzzled, baby head bobbing beside a venerable St. Nicholas.

We are more than halfway through a private baptismal ceremony in Houston for our first grandchild,

Alexander Wesley, called "Sasha," who is the son of our son, Wes, and Iulia, the lovely, intelligent Russian woman he met while working in Moscow on a fellowship in 1993. After a Stanford wedding, they spent a year in the United States, until the homesick bride requested a return to Moscow, where they lived for the next three years. Returning to the States after that, they settled in Austin, which pleased us. However, the birth of her first child stirred longings for Russia in Iulia, so we were grateful when Galina obtained a six-month visa.

I was pleased when Iulia said Galina wanted Sasha to be baptized into the Russian Orthodox faith, for surely the method of baptism doesn't matter to God. But as I stand here (Russian Orthodox churches have no pews) with my husband and Sasha's father and uncle, observers rather than participants, I wonder.

Galina is the baby's godmother, but we've just learned that his other sponsor is the family priest in Moscow, a renowned painter of icons and professor of iconography. My writer self warms to the thought of an artist godparent for Sasha, but my grandmother self worries: With two Russian godparents, if anything should happen to our son and Iulia, would our grandson be raised in Russia? Could I bear that? Yet wouldn't Galina and her husband be equally broken-hearted if Sasha were raised here?

I return my attention to the ceremony. It began an hour earlier with our buying, placing, and lighting candles at several altars. Then we left the church, lined up, and re-entered: priest, warden, Galina and Iulia with Sasha, then the rest of us. Just inside the door, Galina recited a long speech in Russian, a request for baptism, I learned. After the priest responded, we entered the large square room, glowing golden in the November afternoon sun. Lighting the censer, the priest purified this room as well as the sanctuary behind the beautiful carved wooden iconostatis.

After lengthy prayers and readings in Church Slovak came the immersion. Now Galina has carried Sasha back to the center of the room where the priest removes his diaper once again to anoint him from head to foot with an oil used only for baptisms and death. Galina and Iulia rediaper him for the third, or perhaps fourth, time, and pull on a white undershirt on which Iulia has embroidered an ornate red cross.

In a confusion of languages, Galina, who practices English in her e-mails, had described the embroidery as a "dagger," a design she called necessary to make Sasha a "balanced baby." I had thought of Cossacks and worried about a previously undisclosed streak of militancy in Galina's peaceable nature, until Iulia showed me the shirt this morning. "Dagger" referred only to the pointed ends of the cross. Galina drapes a chain with a cross around the baby's wobbly head before she and Iulia finish dressing him. I understand now why Iulia chose playsuits as baptismal garments rather than a keepsake christening dress with a multitude of tiny buttons.

The priest asks Galina a question, she responds "yes," goes to the back of the church, opens the door and spits outside, then returns. We four spectators exchange glances. I can think only that the expectoration must be something like an exorcism; perhaps Galina has taken on the sins of conception and resoundingly expelled them.

The priest carries Sasha gently to a table where he cuts wisps of hair from the baby's head in four different places. He hands them to his mother, symbolizing, I learn later, the permanence of baptism. Still, I'm sorry to see any of his silky hair disappear; momentarily I wish for the routine questions and decorous sprinkling of the five-minute Presbyterian baptisms our sons experienced.

The warden and priest continue chanting prayers, Scripture, and ritual, Church Slovak mostly, but now and then a familiar English phrase. Calmed by the vibration of the chanting, Sasha relaxes in the priest's arms. Then the priest disappears with him through the doors of the iconostatis into the private sanctuary beyond. Galina beckons us to prepare our cameras, and when priest and baby re-emerge, we all take photographs.

Freedom to photograph a sacrament surprises me in this denomination where dress is formal but behavior may not be. Men wear suits and ties; women wear long skirts, never pants, and cover their heads. I had thought about wearing a hat today, but when I saw both Iulia and Galina in headscarves, I tied on a lace mantilla. Yet worshippers may come and go during services as they please, purchase candles or holy pictures, even chat quietly with their neighbors. And as early parishioners arrive for the Saturday night service that follows our baptism, they wander through the ceremony.

The warden turns to us now, indicating with his fingers that there is only an inch or two more of the service remaining. My feet ache after almost an hour and a half of standing, so I'm relieved. After a final series of prayers, Alexander Wesley is presented once more to God, and his baptism is complete.

Smiling, the warden says, "He's really beautiful, and he was very good. Once we baptized seven Gypsy babies. The mothers never stopped screaming, 'You're killing my baby,' and the babies never stopped crying."

I silently praise myself and all of us for our restraint.

Galina, who has been so nervous about the ceremony that she stayed awake most of last night rehearsing her part, finally is able to relax. Beaming, she says, "Sasha is a good baby; my heart is happy."

"Yes," I agree, "my heart is very happy, too."

We embrace. I have grown to love this woman and Sergei, her husband. And I've come to appreciate the strength and faith it took for her to survive the horrors of World War II and for them to recover from the fall of Communism and the decline of their jobs as government scientists. We have been guests at their apartment in Moscow and their dacha outside the city; we believe we know their hearts.

So it really doesn't matter that I didn't understand much of the ceremony of Sasha's baptism. Surely it's premature to worry about who might raise Sasha were something to happen to his parents. Right now he is the epicenter of a circle of people who love him, both Russian and American. What more does he need?

And what more do I need than the sheer wonder of his existence? Just by being born, Sasha has given me the role I've longed for since the marriage of our first son nine years ago. I'm a grandmother. I have someone to read to—Russian and American stories— to play peekaboo with, to hold in my lap and rock, to love when he's with me and when he's away. Now he's with me—and with his Russian grandmother. Arm in arm, we two babushkas leave the church.

—SuzAnne C. Cole

Grumpy and Poopy Doo

ix your own lunch but don't touch the cookies, Bill. They're for the party," she says. "And don't forget to charge the batteries for the video camera. Remember last time?"

The week before Thanksgiving is always busy for us, and the kitchen, with all its celebratory goodies, is off-limits to me this time of year. Our forty-sixth wedding anniversary is the nineteenth of November. Our oldest daughter, Barbara's, birthday falls on the eighteenth. She and her husband, Mark, have two sons. Both were born in November, not the same November; Matt is five and Jake is three. Somewhere along the way, our anniversary got lost in the shuffle. It doesn't matter, though. At our age, a card and a hug and we're done, anyway.

Margaret, my wife, does all the shopping for our two grandsons' birthday presents, with no help from me. The present-buying requires ten trips to the mall and twice that many calls to Barbara. The invasion of Iraq wasn't planned with any more attention to detail.

All shirts must have the proper insignia. Blue's Clues for Matt, Scooby Doo for Jake, and robots and dinosaurs for both. Nothing short of Nike's or Reebok's is acceptable for our grandsons' privileged feet.

The last time I participated in this safari, I went to one store, bought four different kinds of Barney the dinosaur, and went home. I hate shopping, especially this close to Christmas, so I figured I'd get two for each kid. I'd give 'em one each for their birthdays and save the other two for Christmas. Bingo! Job done.

Wrong! That was when I learned that, as far as my hip grandsons were concerned, the pot-bellied, purple reptile had become obsolete. Just as they did eons ago, individual species drop out of the evolutionary toy chain and become extinct so fast that not even a modern Toys-R-Us Charles Darwin could keep up with them.

On the big day, the car is loaded with toys and cookies. I start to get in the car.

Margaret says, "Bill, did you bring the video camera?"

I grumble as I go back to get the camera.

"While you're in there, go to the bathroom," she yells, so loud they could have heard it in Baghdad. "I don't want to have to stop for you."

I return with the camera.

"Bill . . . the door?"

Still grumbling, I walk back and lock it.

The women leave me at Barbara's house with Mark and the boys. They proceed to Tinyland Playworld, where the joint bash for the grandsons is to be held. They go early to deliver the presents, cake, ice cream, and cookies and to give last-minute instructions to the combination director, nursemaid, drill sergeant, and clown who will emcee the festivities.

Mark and I have received orders to bring up the rear in the other car. But first, we are to feed the boys, wash their faces, dress them, and bring the balloons. I'm no good at any of this, except maybe holding balloons.

While Mark is trying to dress the boys, Matt is playing with his new bowling set and yelling for Jake to stop hitting him with one of the pins. Matt threatens, "I've got a booger, and I'm not afraid to use it."

Mark says, "Don't hit your brother in the head, Jake, I just combed his hair."

Then he asks Jake, "Are you poopy again?"

"No poopy!" Jake tries an end-run past me.

I grab him by his Scooby Doo T-shirt and sniff. "Yep, he's poopy."

"Change him, will you, Pop?" Mark says. "I've got my hands full."

"Okay. Come on, Poopy Doo," I say.

After bungling the diaper job on the squirming kid, I sit on the couch holding the balloons and wishing my son-in-law would at least keep a couple of beers in the fridge.

Tinyland is located in the middle of a little strip center in the western part of town. The mothers start to arrive with their little rug-rats and toddlers in tow, each with a gift and assorted communicable diseases, snotty noses, and individual agendas, none of which, fortunately, include me. Matt and Jake immediately organize the other miscreants in a systematic destruction of the play equipment.

With the chatter of mothers and the screams of children, delighted and otherwise, in our ears, Mark and I dutifully go about setting up lights, tripods, and cameras to record this historic epic on film and video for replaying ad nauseum on Christmas Eve for all the kinfolks. Mark's face suddenly takes on an expression of panic.

"Cover me, Pop. I forgot film."

While Mark slips out to buy film, I smugly go about setting up my video camera, safely protected by the armor of long years of experience.

The director looks like a fat Ronald McDonald. She screeches, "Okay, munchkins. Let's all put on our happy faces and sing 'Happy Birthday' to our birthday boys."

I've been to these little productions before, and each time, I could swear that woman sneaks out to the kitchen for a nip.

At the first chord of "Happy Birthday" I discover my battery is dead. Quick-thinking veteran that I am, I continue pointing my camera and acting as if nothing's happened.

Some kid does something cute, and Margaret turns to me. "Did you get that?"

"Of course, I did; don't be ridiculous." I casually fake taking more pictures, careful not to reveal to her that the red light is off.

When her attention is attracted elsewhere, I race back to my bag to see if I had packed the spare battery. I hadn't. I return and pretend to shoot every outrageous act my grandsons perform. I wrack my brain for possible ways to blame this on Mark. None comes to mind.

Margaret looks around. "Where's Mark?"

"Oh, you know our dumb son-in-law," I say in superior self-righteousness. "He forgot to bring film."

I am rescued from further interrogation by the entrance of the "other" grandma. Wife immediately puts on her game face.

"Now, honey," I caution. "Don't start that who's-the-favorite-grandma routine again. Remember, we've got to eat at her house on Christmas. You mess with her, and she'll demote you to green beans again."

My daughter walks up to me. "Where's Mark?"

"Uh, he had an emergency at the office. It'll just take a few minutes."

"He forgot the film again, didn't he?" she says.

By the time Mark returns, I have given up faux-filming and am standing around, feeling lost and wondering if my daughter's forced smile is hurting her face.

After an animated, whispered conversation with Mark, Barbara turns on me. "Don't lurk, Daddy," she says. "You're scaring the children."

The other fathers begin to magically receive urgent calls on their cell phones and quickly take their leave. Why didn't I think of that?

All the chairs are made for dwarfs and Barbie dolls. I am wondering why they provide chairs for kids who never sit down, yet they have none for old guys like me who spend half their time in the bathroom and the rest looking for some other place to sit.

Cake and ice cream are served. The little delin-quents sit down and start throwing the stuff at each other. The Birthday Boys blow out their candles and stick them in each other's ears. By this time, I'm not the only one looking at his watch, and the painted smile on the director's clown face is slipping perceptively.

I find a bench and watch Jake opening presents and screaming with delight. My younger grandson has a streak of chocolate from his chin up to his left ear, and melted ice cream soaks the entire front of his Scooby Doo T-shirt.

Cool, big brother Matt is off somewhere playing with his three little girlfriends: Katelyn, Kaitlin, and Kaitland.

Jake looks up and spots me watching him. He cocks his little three-year-old head and gives me a smile that would light up the Eiffel tower. He toddles over to me, holds up his sticky hands, and says, "Grandpa!" like he has just realized for the first time that I am there. He crawls up onto my lap, swings his little legs back and forth, and smiles at me again. Then he leans over, rests his head on my chest, and falls asleep.

With melting ice cream soaking my shirt, I hold him very still until the hubbub subsides. Then, feeling more important than I have in years, I carry my exhausted little grandson out and strap him into his car seat. I kiss him on the forehead and whisper, "Happy birthday, little guy. You made my day."

—*William M. Barnes*

A Valentine
for a Neat Kid

David became a member of our family when his mother, Rose, married our son, Curt. At their wedding, David, a handsome, blond toddler dressed in a miniature tuxedo, expressed himself with piercing little cries. He didn't smile or respond to anyone for more than a few seconds. At every attempt to hug or touch him, he pulled away, screaming. This set him apart from the other children and caused whispering and raised eyebrows among the guests.

David was our first grandson, and I offered to care for him while the newlyweds took a short honeymoon. It didn't take long for the experience to exhaust me. In constant motion when awake, he rocked back and forth or raced about the house, leaping on and off the furniture. I admit to being relieved when Curt and Rose returned.

The little family moved into a small home with a fenced yard, and David gradually changed from acting like a small screaming dervish to just a noisy, active little boy. Surprising everyone, he learned to talk and responded to toilet training. Tranquil surroundings relaxed David's bland expression, especially when he sat in his small red rocker holding a battered teddy bear. He still wouldn't allow cuddling, even from his mother.

After a year and a half, David's interim of contentment in his first stable home evaporated. Severe bipolar illness struck his mother. Rose's wide mood swings and occasional violent episodes fractured the marriage and made her unable to care for David. The four-year-old became a ward of the court.

Curt had not adopted David, but the Department of Social Services urged him to become the child's legal guardian until Rose's mental condition stabilized. With my husband's and my encouragement, Curt accepted this arrangement, because the alternatives for David were a series of foster homes or an institution. Curt began a long search for day care, but found none available for an emotionally challenged child like David.

I knew someone must care for David while our son worked to support them, but after raising five children as a stay-at-home mother, I had taken a job I enjoyed very much. I hated to give up my new independence to begin more days of child rearing. Martyrdom surfaced, followed by guilt for it, but thinking of David's few alternatives stiffened my resolve and I gave up my outside job.

Doubt over my ability to cope with David nagged at me most. By then, he had been diagnosed as autistic, and he existed in a world alien to others and to me. David rarely actually spoke to anyone, yet he talked to himself constantly, usually in a loud voice, parroting the conversations of people around him, television shows, or commercials, complete with full sound effects. If I scolded him mildly, David repeated my words at the exact decibel of my voice—for days. His echoing, interspersed with frequent nerve-shattering shrieks, continued. He played out imaginary scenes while he twirled sticks or twisted a drinking straw with his fingers. Regular temper tantrums sent him writhing and screaming to the floor. A social worker told me that these outbursts stemmed from David's frustration with being unable to bridge the gap between his inner world and the world around him. To David, normal sensory experiences were often confusing and overwhelming.

I tried each day to penetrate the shield David pulled around himself by reading or telling him stories and taking him for rides in my van. I talked to David while I did my housework, and to entertain him while I made him peanut butter sandwiches, his favorite lunch, I whistled and made silly comments, like "whew!" and "rats!" He repeated my words, but he didn't converse and he never laughed.

One day during a terrible tantrum, David pounded me with his fists and screamed himself into exhaustion. I collapsed into a chair, feeling drained and defeated, and prayed for guidance. I had learned to speak to him in a low, calm voice to ease his tantrums. This time, my calming words had no effect, so I sang "I'm a Little Teapot." David sat up and listened, and then repeated the song several times. That evening, Curt bought him a turntable and tape player, and I got out records accumulated during my children's early years. Curt showed David how to operate the player himself. David listened to the songs over and over, twirling his straw and rocking.

Curt came home from work one day excited about a special program that David's mother had investigated before her own illness had become crippling. The Experimental Education program at the University of Washington accepted David into their program, and I drove him there several times a week. I watched through a one-way window as the staff of trained specialists for developmentally delayed and autistic children worked with the small group. During the first several sessions, David just twirled his drinking straw and showed no interest in the activities. Then one day he responded to the instructors by producing a nearly perfect drawing of a school bus. He signed it "David." I wept. I had not known he could print his name. A locked door had opened.

David responded well to treatment, surprising and encouraging his counselors, and he slowly but steadily improved. He began to speak, rather than just parrot. After five years of psychiatric counseling and training in the Experimental Education program, David entered the special education program of our local school district.

At age ten, David could use a computer with ease, read at high-school level, and had handwriting better than Curt's. He could not fathom the school's written examinations, so they tested him orally. Because his social and communicative skills had not caught up with his intellectual level, David remained in a sheltered classroom until junior high. Several times I had to rush to school to bring him home when he grew frustrated over something, but with each year, his tantrums became increasingly rare. He still talked to himself and twirled straws, but the other children were more accepting than most adults.

David learned to ride a bicycle, swim, and fish from Curt's boat. When Curt volunteered to help with Special Olympics, David decided to compete in several sports. He has a large collection of winning ribbons, and he still competes in Special Olympic events.

When he reached his teens, David asked to be called "Dave," a name he obviously thought gave him a more mature status. I was pleased with his growing independence and how he would ask questions and initiate conversations. His favorite activity was joining our family for special dinners and holidays. He pored over our picture albums, especially those of Curt and Rose's wedding, as if he wanted to secure his place among us. I made a special album just for him.

Over the years, David's mother improved with treatment and became well enough to take him every other weekend and for special occasions. Curt always interviewed Rose before taking David to her house, knowing she occasionally refused to take her medication. On those occasions when his mother suffered a severe mood swing during his visit, David required special attention when he returned home. Counselors told Curt that David had to learn to deal with his mother's mental condition—a heavy assignment for any child, much less one with a neurobiological disability such as autism. But, with the help of his counselors, parents, and grandparents, David managed pretty well.

The years passed quickly, and then David turned nineteen and we received his high school graduation announcement. Curt, David's mother, grandmother, and one of his aunts, and my husband and I attended. We arrived a little late, and the stifling ninety-degree heat followed us inside. The only remaining seats were in the bleacher section, where we wedged ourselves among many teenage friends of the graduates.

During the ceremony, I was more anxious than I'd been at any of my five children's graduations. As the processional began, a teacher handed a long-stemmed red rose to each boy. I wondered what part the flowers would play and worried: *Would David follow the plan? Could he move through the ritual without becoming upset?* The graduates walked to their assigned seats in pairs, and I smiled as Dave searched and found us in the crowd and waved. He sat through the musical renditions and speeches, twirling a small straw with one hand and clasping the rose stem with the other.

Another suffocating hour passed while diplomas were presented. David's turn came near the last. When the superintendent of schools called him by his favorite title, "Dave B," a rustling arose and the entire audience stood and clapped. No one else, not even the honor students, had received such a resounding ovation. My eyes and those of many others filled with tears.

I asked the young girl beside me, "Why did they do that for David?"

She answered, "Because Dave is the neatest kid in school. Everyone likes him."

At the recessional, the boys handed the roses to their girl partners, and the couples filed out. With my tissue sodden and tears still squeezing from my eyes, I followed the graduates to the courtyard. David's six-feet-three height towered above his classmates as he strode rapidly toward us. He still carried a rose. When he reached our group, he handed the flower to his mother, who smiled through her tears.

"Weren't you supposed to give the rose to the girl, Dave? She'll be disappointed," Rose said.

"Miss Canby gave me two roses, Mom. One for you and one for Angela."

Following graduation, David spent a year in a group home for special young adults, but both he and Curt were miserable until David moved back to his old home. He still lives with our son and works at a well-known restaurant as a cook's helper, a job he has held for eight years. He rides a bus to work and keeps in touch with all of us by cellular phone.

David loves flying with Curt in his Cessna 150, though he often gets airsick. He enjoys watching the latest DVD movies and surfing the Internet. The small twirling straw has been replaced with a Walkman playing his favorite rock music. Schedules are important to autistic people, and David does not like to have them interrupted. He would be lost without a good watch and a calendar. David is both trustworthy and trusting, but Curt feels he cannot be entirely on his own, because others might intrude on his benevolent personality.

David never forgets anyone he has ever met, he knows where they work, and he remembers the names of their family members. He never forgets family birthdays and anniversaries. He always calls me on my birthday and, to my chagrin, he always knows just how old I am. When I give him presents, he calls or writes his thanks immediately. He is the only one of my eleven grandchildren who still sends me valentines.

David became a part of my life first as a necessary addition to my family, then as a difficult challenge, and finally as a wonderful blessing. This thoughtful, handsome "neat kid" is my very special valentine, and I am honored to be his grandmother.

—Mary Brockway

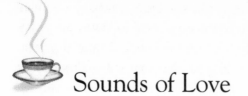

Sounds of Love

H i, Mom. Do you have anything planned for Wednesday morning?" The cheerful voice on the other end of the line belonged to my daughter, Kerry.

"Not yet," I answered, "Wednesday's free. Why, did you have something in mind?"

"How would you like to spend some time with me?" she asked. "I'll pop for lunch."

"Sounds too good to turn down. Are we celebrating something?"

"Could be. I'll pick you up at nine-fifteen."

Accustomed to her surprises, I didn't get too curious over her ambiguous invitation. She picked me up on Wednesday morning, and after a short ride she drove into a parking lot with a sign identifying a gynecology and obstetrical medical clinic. She hadn't mentioned any female problems or starting a family.

Excited that it might be the latter, I waited for a clue, but she didn't volunteer any, so I followed her inside and sat on a chair while she checked in at the desk.

After Kerry disappeared from the waiting room, I listened to soft classical music piped over the intercom. A music lover, I relaxed and thought how often in my life I have been comforted by sound— the sounds of music, nature, and endearing voices. I closed my eyes and fantasized how wonderful it would be to become a grandmother.

My reverie ended when I heard Kerry's voice, "Good news, Mom. You're going to be a grand-mother."

"Say it again," I urged.

"You're going to be a grandmother . . . next spring."

Her words sounded like a symphony. Elated, I jumped to my feet, eager to sing an aria proclaiming my good news to the world. Instead, I smiled into the smiling faces of the other patients and left.

I can't remember any time in my life when I didn't love children. Years earlier, when doctors cautioned me that I might not ever bear children, I was devastated. Thankfully, their predictions did not come true. My husband and I were the overjoyed parents of three children. Being a mother was one of the highlights of my life. Now I was going to be a grandmother!

Over the next months, Kerry and I spent hours shopping for furniture and browsing in infant departments, debating what colors and clothes to select for the baby's layette.

Then came alarming news reports in the media. Expectant mothers who had taken the prescription drug thalidomide were delivering babies with birth defects. Fears that other prescription and over-the-counter medications might also pose a risk to pregnant women and their unborn children flowed throughout the world. Stunned, we reviewed any medications Kerry had taken. We tossed aside negative thoughts about birth defects and said prayers thanking God in advance for a healthy baby. Our excitement increased when Kerry's baby began kicking. Sometimes, we smoothed our hands over her belly and talked to our heir in hopes of proving the theory that fetuses can recognize voices. We also talked, sang, and laughed to the baby as if we were already holding him or her in our arms.

Because my mother preferred raising boys, I grew up in my brothers' shadows. So when I became a mother of daughters, I showered them with all the love I felt I had missed. Now, it seemed natural to wish for a granddaughter. Of course, I never expressed my choice aloud, knowing that I'd welcome a baby of either gender. Occasionally I asked Kerry, "Wouldn't it be nice if we had a little girl, just like you?"

Winter passed. And on a sunny spring day, my husband and I sat in the maternity ward at the hospital, eagerly waiting to become grandparents. He had been out of town on business trips during the birth of our first two children, so he made sure he was available for our grandchild's birth.

Because her baby was not positioned right for birthing, Kerry was given an epidural to ease her pain.

Like thousands before us, we waited apprehensively for what seemed an eternity until, finally, a nurse returned with news that we had a healthy grandbaby.

"Is it a girl?" I asked expectantly.

Flashing a smile instead of an answer, she led us down a corridor. Just as we turned a corner and faced doors to the delivery room, they swung open. Kerry was wheeled out on a gurney, her face aglow with a triumphant smile. Her husband stood beside her, holding an infant wrapped in a coverlet.

"You have a granddaughter," he said proudly. He opened the blanket and showed us a magnificently formed little girl. "We've named her Kristine."

I looked into my grandbaby's cherubic face and watched her tiny blue eyes open and her delicate pink lips curve into a half moon. "Isn't she beautiful?" I cried. Knowing hospital sanitation regulations, I resisted the urge to take Kristine into my arms and cuddle her close. But I couldn't restrain my enthusiasm. "I'm so happy. I wanted a girl."

During the next two years, Kristine grew from a happy baby wearing a peach fuzz hairstyle into an active toddler with a blonde ponytail. Being the typical first-time grandmother, I boasted about every word she uttered, every step she took, and every cute thing she said or did, until our patient and more experienced friends reminded me that their grandchildren had said and done similar things.

One day when Kristine had graduated from words to sentences, she climbed up on my lap, hugged me, and looked into my eyes as if peering into my soul. "Grandma, I love you," she said, and kissed me. "I'm so glad you wanted me."

Puzzling over her words, I returned her hugs. The warmth of her tiny body brought back memories of talking to her in the womb and my enthusiastic outburst upon seeing her for the first time: "I wanted a girl."

That's when I knew that sounds of love are not only heard. They're also remembered.

—*Sally Kelly-Engeman*

The Land of That's Okay

Our son, Willy, scrambled out of the car and ran full-throttle into his grandparents' home—before we could unload our suitcases or lure any gummy worms or M&Ms from the cracks and crevices of the backseat. Stopping only long enough for quick hello hugs and kisses, he darted through the living room and climbed onto Grandma's organ bench. He teetered on the edge of the padded leather seat, stretching until his chubby little fingers reached and flipped the shiny silver toggle switch. The organ started purring quietly, but not for long. Willy's squeals of delight increased in direct proportion to the velocity and volume of the randomly played notes as he pressed one key after another in typical toddler fashion.

We had approached the trip with apprehension, fearing the antics of a two-year-old were too chaotic and too intrusive for his grandparents. They weren't accustomed to having small children in their home for an entire week, let alone one with Willy's energy and enthusiasm for life.

As soon as Willy began to play, our parental apprehensions collided with his grandparents' appreciation of being able to spend time with their youngest grandson. We urged our little music maker, "Play quietly and gently." Almost instantly our stated intentions to restore some semblance of serenity to the household were followed by Grandpa's utterance of, "Oh, that's okay. He can't hurt the organ, and his music sounds good to me."

We should have remembered from previous trips that they could see beyond the inconvenience, the schedule interruptions, the fingerprints on the glass door, and the potential for broken knickknacks and carpet stains. We had forgotten how much they loved claiming the gift of the moment, a gift they could only open twice a year because of the miles between us.

After reaching the end of his spontaneous musical overture, Willy climbed off the organ bench, toddled across the living room, pulled a cardboard box from the back of the coat closet to the middle of the room, and dumped all the toys out of it. There were not a lot of toys in the box, but they created quite an obstacle course in the living room once scattered about. Because of the room's central location in the house, my husband and I were concerned about maintaining a pathway through the newly constructed indoor playground. "Put some toys back in the box or at least move them out of the way," we coaxed. "We don't want Grandpa and Grandma to trip on the toys and fall down."

Immediately Grandpa said, "Oh, that's okay. Those toys are here to be played with. Let him enjoy them."

Willy's constant demands to have Grandpa and Grandma play with him also began shortly after our arrival. We enjoyed watching him move from one grandparent's lap to another, working his wide-eyed magic and cute little smile to entice them into a game of peekaboo, to read him a story, or to turn the cylindrical toy filled with bright colored beads over one more time so he could watch them cascade through the sorting holes. When we decided the grandparents had probably endured enough play time, we calmly stated, "Willy, you need to let Grandpa and Grandma rest for a while."

"Oh, that's okay. I'm not tired yet," Grandpa assured us. Grandma smiled in agreement, and both continued to participate in whatever games Willy selected.

Spotting a plate of Grandma's homemade oatmeal raisin cookies on the kitchen counter, Willy parted the sea of toys and headed straight for the tempting treats. Thinking it only natural to invoke the same set of rules by which we were raised, we instructed, "Son, don't eat anything now. We'll be eating supper soon."

Grandpa instantly countered with, "Oh, that's okay. He must be hungry, and a few cookies won't hurt anything."

Accepting the fact that the no-snacks-so-close-to-a-meal rule was temporarily suspended, we decided we should at least encourage Willy to stay in the kitchen to eat the cookies. But as he headed toward the living room, leaving a trail of crumbs on the white carpet, and before we could comment, Grandpa said, "That's okay. We can always vacuum."

The rest of the week at Grandma and Grandpa's house unfolded just as it had every other time we'd visited them. We started out apprehensive. Willy and both grandparents started out embracing the moment. By the end of the week, the new rules were established and accepted by all.

Over the next several years, we came to affectionately call this harmless change in routine "The Land of That's Okay." We knew part of the joy of each trip was letting Grandpa and Grandma shower Willy with unconditional love, including a slight suspension of the normal rules of childhood.

Our visits to The Land of That's Okay ended with equal predictability. We stuffed suitcases back into the car trunk, restocked the backseat snack container with juice boxes and a gallon-size zip-lock bag full of Grandma's homemade cookies, said tearful goodbyes, and backed out of their driveway. Within a few minutes of starting our journey home, we told Willy, as pleasantly as we could, "We are leaving The Land of That's Okay and going back home. Daddy's and Mommy's rules must be followed again." By the time we arrived home, the leniencies and unmerited favor shown to Willy by his grandparents were memories he could cherish, but he was fully aware that the rules of his own home were different and back in place.

One of our pilgrimages to The Land of That's Okay, where Grandpa was chief rule maker and establisher of new routines, was made about a month before his death. Grandpa was not in good health at the time, but he still did what he could to make the visit special and to give Willy a break from the normal rules and routines of home.

Hospice workers came and went while we were there. Neighbors and relatives stopped in to see how Grandpa was doing, knowing that future visits were very unlikely. Grandpa couldn't play as much, and we had to be a little quieter than on previous trips. Still, it was one more special time for Willy and his grandpa. It was one more trip to The Land of That's Okay that will always be cherished.

The death of someone you love is never easy, even when it is obviously imminent, as in Grandpa's case the last time we saw him. It was painful to tell Willy that Grandpa had died, but we embraced him and told him that Grandpa was now in heaven. We told him heaven is a wonderful place where Grandpa will spend forever doing the things he loves to do, where rules aren't necessary, and where he will always be happy. But it was Willy's memories, not our reassuring words, that provided his greatest source of comfort. He knew his grandpa would be just fine in heaven. After all, it was Grandpa himself who had given him an idea of what heaven might be like during our semi-annual, weeklong vacations to The Land of That's Okay.

—*Valerie Kay Gwin*

Love-a-Bye

B race yourself," I whispered to my friend Patricia. "Here comes Ed with another hundred pictures of his new grandson."

New grandparents were an enigma to me. They gushed with exuberance about birth weights and accomplishments, like turning over and sitting up—all of which were done earlier and better than any other child ever born.

"I now have six hundred pictures of little Eddie posted on his Web site," Ed boasted.

"How could the birth of a grandchild top the birth of one's own children?" I wondered.

Then it was my turn.

Over the objections of my daughter's physicians, she decided to have a baby. Megan had a scary medical history with a brain aneurysm and seizures by the time she was twenty-four, but she was determined.

Reminiscent of the outspoken Ouiser Boudreaux in *Steel Magnolias*, I cursed and raved to no avail. Like the movie's strong-willed Shelby, Megan desperately wanted her own child no matter what the personal cost to her might be.

Within a few months of her campaign to conceive, she came by to tell me she was pregnant—and that she needed to move in with me. Her fiancé wasn't ready to be a parent, and they had broken their engagement. Stunned, I agreed she should come back home. Thus began an incredible venture that would take us through months of morning sickness that pared forty pounds off Megan's thin body and a series of trying decisions that too often elicited the question of abortion.

During those early and difficult months, the doctors told us the baby was a girl. We also learned there was a good possibility she would have Down's syndrome, and that she might have spina bifida and a cleft palate. Megan would have to face these challenges as a single parent, but she was adamant. Her baby was a keeper.

Immersed within a maze of special vitamins and medications, weekly blood tests, and frequent ultrasounds, we labored though the days, trying to work and keep smiling. Every new test seemed to bring more challenging decisions to make. The doctors were clear: Megan's pregnancy was extremely dangerous to her health and the baby's. The odds that one or both of them would die were enormous.

My prayers took on an urgent pleading beyond anything I had ever experienced. My total attention was on my daughter, whom I desperately loved and was terrified I would lose. I was cautious about loving the baby she proudly carried. *What if Megan died or had the stroke the doctors kept warning us about? What if this baby was severely handicapped? Would we have the physical and financial resources to provide for her? Would I blame my granddaughter if my daughter died bringing her into the world? Could I raise another child as an over-fifty grandmother?*

Megan's labor went on for a torturous forty-eight hours. I wanted the doctors to go ahead with a C-section, but Megan rejected the idea every time it was raised. I refused to sleep as she labored. I had to be there every minute. Beyond logic, I believed it was imperative for me to be vigilant, as though I could protect my child from whatever was going to happen.

My son, Will, and I had agreed ahead of time that he would stay with his sister and I would go with the baby if there were any complications. We lived on a small island in Hawaii, and if any serious problems were to occur, one or both of them would have to be airlifted to a specialty hospital on Oahu.

We finally reached the summit when an exhausted Megan gave birth to a beautiful baby girl—nine pounds of solid love. Will cut the cord and placed his sister's new daughter in her arms.

"She has your ears," he showed Megan.

Within minutes of her birth, the baby began gasping for air and was rushed to the nursery for oxygen and evaluation. At the same time, Megan began hemorrhaging. Will and I stuck to our plan. I went to the nursery; he stayed with his sister. While the respiratory technician hooked up oxygen, the nurses briskly rubbed my new granddaughter with towels, trying to stimulate her and get a healthy cry. Mesmerized with fear, I watched as the nurse laid her flaccid body in the bassinette. Instinctively, she turned her small head toward the oxygen vent and took a deep breath. I wept with joy as she eagerly sucked in the life-giving air with her perfect, tiny mouth.

Back in the labor room, the IV medications and the fast work of her obstetrician had halted Megan's hemorrhage. The grace of God was with us, and within an hour, they both had stabilized.

My granddaughter, Anne, had no visible signs of physical defect, but based on the pediatrician's recommendation, when she was twelve days old we flew her to Oahu to be evaluated by several specialists. The orthopedic surgeon told us she had hip dysplasia, which meant her legs turned in too much. Another surgeon told us she was tongue-tied, which might require surgery later. The cardiologist found two holes in her heart and pulmonary valve dysfunction, which would most likely require open-heart surgery around age six.

Our hearts ached, yet through it all, Anne smiled and thrived. I had the sense she knew more than we did; maybe an angel had whispered a message in her tiny ear.

The magnitude of love and pride flowing in my heart for my granddaughter was overwhelming. Like a first love, I held her and smelled her and rocked her as if in a trance.

"Don't teach her bad habits," Megan would caution me as I taught Anne to stick out her tongue to stretch her frenulum, the piece of skin that holds our tongues to the floor of our mouths. It worked, and she now has perfect speech (not average, you understand).

At ten months, Anne had her first kidney infection. So, off to another specialist we flew. She was under mild anesthesia for a series of procedures that revealed her kidneys weren't functioning correctly. She would probably need kidney surgery by the time she was three. In the meantime, each infection would be treated with antibiotics.

Broken-hearted that my daughter would be a single parent as I had been for fifteen years, I determined to carve out a path so wide and so clear, it would light their way. In addition to my regular job, I started a small business to bring in extra income. We made arrangements for Megan to return to the university to complete her degree. I bought insurance policies, prepared a new will, and established a personal trust.

What I didn't know and couldn't have known was that my granddaughter didn't need me to clear a path for her. She would be lighting the way for me.

Within a year, I was forced to retire on a disability. Distraught and embarrassed, I sulked and tried to withdraw. However, Anne refused to attend my pity party. She was there every morning and night to spur me onward. It didn't matter that I wasn't interested in food; she was. I could be disheveled, but she wanted clean diapers. I could sit and stare at the TV, but Anne was on the move, scooting from one room to another as fast as her chubby legs could carry her. Some days, it seemed she was jet-propelled. But above all, she loved me unabashedly. With time, I began to realize my granddaughter would be the lifeline to my new future.

Through many a thicket, we have laughed, loved, and tumbled our way down new paths, praying as we went. My retirement provided me with the privilege of being home with my grandchild. We bake cookies and grow flowers together. I help at school, assist with homework, and sew frilly dresses. We sing and dance and do all those things that were so challenging when I worked full-time and raised my children single-handedly.

Anne has my dark brown eyes and the thick dark eyelashes I always wanted to trade my blonde ones for. Slowly and miraculously, she has healed. After exercises and triple diapering to straighten her hips, her legs are fine and strong. Her kidneys are clear and functioning without surgery. The two holes in her heart have mended. There is still a possibility of heart surgery, but now it can be managed with a less complicated procedure. I'm convinced an angel has been with her since she was conceived.

One of Anne's first words was "love-a-bye," her pronunciation of "lullaby," which she often requested. I sang her many love-a-byes, often changing the words to include her name, her likes, and her dislikes. Thankfully, she has ignored the fact that I can't carry a tune in a bucket. One day when she was almost two, I held her tiny hand in mine as we snuggle-buggled at nap time. I was stricken with the enormity of the inexplicable cord that connected our souls. My granddaughter, lying next to me, grasping her "gankie" (pink blanket) and falling into the deep sleep of a contented child, was the mysterious gift of life that God had shared with me.

Being free from the daily tedium of long work hours outside the home has permitted me to concentrate, really concentrate, on sharing her life. We pause to study leaves, worms, and ladybugs. We make stained-glass windows out of tissue paper and glue, finger-paint, play softball, go to the park, and giggle our way to sleep telling knock-knock jokes. Her jokes make no sense to anyone else, but I find them hilarious, or "ilarious," as she says.

People frequently comment on her beauty. Of course, one hates to brag; but she is, indeed, beautiful—smart and creative, too. Unlike my children, she loves many of the things I do. She cracks the eggs and measures ingredients as we cook together. She loves gardening, especially digging in the dirt. She's doing needlepoint, but above all, she adores reading and books. She loves science books. Did I mention I'm a registered nurse?

I've been an avid reader since I was a child, and for years I did technical writing and health care pieces for magazines while trudging forward on the proverbial novel. A few years ago, Megan suggested I try my hand at children's books, and I love it. I have ready-made critics in Anne and her classmates. I love lingering in the library with Anne, revisiting children's classics and new books. She now writes in her own version of a journal. She will, no doubt, be a bestselling author.

As you might have guessed, I, too, gush with pride when I discuss my granddaughter. The latest snapshots are always in my wallet and her accomplishments on the tip of my tongue. I cried when she memorized the "Pledge of Allegiance" and wiped tears when she was the star that led the wise men to the stable in Bethlehem. I am still sometimes shocked at how unconditionally, completely, and irreversibly bound in love I am with this wonderful child.

When my granddaughter first entered my life, I wondered how it would all work out, given her fragile beginning and medical challenges and the loss of my health and profession. Now, I am simply in wonder . . . of her. What happiness and purpose she has brought to my life. I couldn't ask for a more rewarding job than that of grandmother—the devoted, off-key singer of made-to-order love-a-byes, just for Anne.

—*Mahala Church*

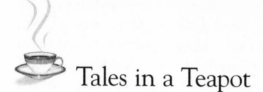

Tales in a Teapot

Of all the teapots in my collection, Grandma's is the one I'm least likely to use when my neighbor and I sit down to visit. It's not a very pretty teapot. The flowers painted on its front look like something a child drew, and its off-white glazed coating appears dirty next to the translucent shimmer of my porcelain teapots. When I serve tea to my friends, I'm more likely to reach for the teapot decorated with dainty roses. It reminds me of the Victorian era, when women sat in lacy dresses and flowered hats.

But when my four-year-old daughter and I "take tea," I choose Grandma's teapot every time. Our parties are lavishly laid out on the floor of her bedroom, complete with cloth napkins and china plates. She sits with three strings of brightly colored beads around her neck, a jeweled tiara on her head, and

Cinderella slippers on her feet. Her back straight, her pinkie finger extended, she begins our tea party with the regal elegance of Queen Victoria.

"Lovely day we're having, wouldn't you agree?" she says, her head tilted just so and her lips slightly pursed.

"Why, yes, it is. I do believe it is the prettiest day this week," I say. "May I pour you a cup of tea?"

"Oh, yes. Thank you, m'dear. I do so like the way you have prepared today's refreshments."

We fill our plates with grapes and vanilla wafers, and, in our best English accents, we continue discussing the weather and how it affects our plans for the rest of the day. After a sip of our chocolate milk "tea," my daughter delicately dabs her lips with a napkin and lays her hands in her lap.

"What a pretty teapot you've chosen for today's party," she says. "It's Grandma's, isn't it?"

"Well, actually, this is my grandma's—your great-grandma's—teapot."

She frowns and wrinkles her nose, trying to picture a woman she has never met.

"The grandma who had to pull feathers out of chickens?" She has dropped her pretend voice of royalty and is looking at me intently, waiting for more of an explanation.

"Yes," I say, "that grandma." And together we imagine what it was like to raise chickens and collect eggs, deciding that it must have been a smelly, messy job. Then we talk about how different life would be without microwaves, computers, and DVDs. I tell her that Great-Grandma made some of the quilts we wrap around us when we watch TV and that the chocolate cake she likes so much is Great-Grandma's recipe.

"I wish I could have met her." She sighs, then quickly brightens. "But I have my grandma. Did she pull feathers out of chickens, too?"

I'm pretty sure she did, but we decide to call and ask. Within a few seconds, she's retrieved the cordless phone from my bedroom and is asking for the number.

"Hi, Grandma. We're having a tea party. Did you pull feathers out of chickens like Mom's grandma did?" She stops to take a breath, and her eyes widen as she listens to Grandma's response.

"You did? Really?" She flashes me a smile.

"They chased you around the yard? That's funny! Did they ever catch you?"

Then her voice turns serious. "No. I wouldn't like that either. I'd be scared, too."

With the chicken-plucking question answered, their conversation turns present-day. I listen as my daughter describes every detail of our tea party, from the napkins and the food to her tiara and the yellow hat I'm wearing.

"That's your hat?" she shrieks into the phone. She turns to me and cries "Mom! Grandma used to wear that hat to church!"

I sense another story coming through the phone lines, another series of questions, answers, and laughter. Their conversation lasts five minutes longer. After saying good bye, she hands me the phone and in her most serious voice reports that Grandma told her to call anytime she wants to learn more about chickens.

I always knew Grandma's teapot had a place in my collection, but now I have a better understanding of where it fits. It's filled with stories that link my family of today with our family of yesterday.

As a child, I spent many of my Sunday afternoons visiting Grandma and Grandpa. My mom, dad, brother, and I would arrive in time for a noontime meal of baked ham or chicken casserole, homemade rye bread, and Jell-O salad. Our dinner-table conversations about day-to-day school and church activities gradually shifted to stories about family. I heard stories about immigrants from Sweden, relatives in Washington, and a great-uncle who died when he was a teenager. Our leisurely meal was punctuated with laughter and frequent interruptions to find a picture in the photo album.

My daughter lives 250 miles from her grandma, and our Sunday afternoons are spent on the soccer field. Our e-mail messages and phone conversations are usually short and to-the-point. They're newsy— we report on the week's activities and outline the calendar's agenda for next week—but they're quiet. There's no laughter, no back-and-forth peppering of questions, no segues to family stories of the past. Grandma's teapot offers that segue.

I suspect Queen Victoria would have frowned at the chocolate milk moustache that adorns my daughter's face, but I know both my grandma and her grandma would have smiled. Then they would have poured another cup.

So I delicately dab my lips, extend my pinkie finger, and ask my daughter to pass the vanilla wafers. And we begin a new story.

—Karna J. Converse

Pieces of Eight

Eight granddaughters! Not bad for an only daughter of an only daughter. I began my tenure as a grandmother at the age of forty-two when my oldest son, Vince, announced Amanda's impending arrival. I protested I was too young to be a grandmother; I was still too busy being a mother. I had a daughter in high school and I was preparing for my second son's wedding. Besides, I had a full-time job, volunteered at church, and was a part-time university student, trying to earn my degree in business. I thought of a quotation I had heard somewhere: "A grandmother is one who has time." When would I have time?

It happened insidiously. One morning several years later I found myself snuggled in among the pillows with two giggling girls, reading a story, accompanied by extremely high-pitched squeals. Amanda's debut had been closely followed by that of her sister, Sarah. I read some more, and we giggled; then I read some more, and we giggled and giggled. I suddenly realized I was having the time of my life. It didn't matter that I had all those other things to do, all those obligations to fulfill. What mattered was here and now and two laughing granddaughters.

Through the years, that lesson has been reinforced numerous times. One summer Amanda, who once described herself as orange (excited) and purple (happy), and Sarah, whose color is anything bright, bold, and eclectic, were visiting. They were getting a little bored as I scurried about doing adult things. *A grandmother is one who has time*; the thought dropped unbidden into my mind. Having just bought a video camera, another idea popped into my head. "Let's make a movie." Thus began a wild, happy afternoon, filled with the unexpected. We devised costumes, searched out props, rearranged furniture to make appropriate scenes, and semi-learned how to operate the video camera. The result? A tape suitable for *America's Funniest Home Videos* and an unforgettable memory.

Heather entered my life when Vince remarried. She was six years old, blond, blue-eyed, and nicknamed "PeeWee." She was somewhat tentative with me, not exactly shy, just unsure. Though I was eager to get to know my new daughter-in-law, I decided to spend time with my new granddaughter. I invited Heather for a walk, and soon we were gathering wild flowers and catching grasshoppers. Before I knew it, she was talking a mile a minute, a trait that has only intensified with time. I fell in love with her immediately and recognized that now-familiar feeling of knowing that catching those grasshoppers was the most important thing in the world at that moment.

My son Pat presented me with granddaughters also. Caroline was a sensitive and intense child, belying her flaming red hair. Once, when asked if anyone else in her family had red hair, she thought for a minute and said, "Yes, my dog." Her sister, Molly, just fourteen months younger, can best be described as a tornado—a whirling, seemingly nonstop bundle of energy, which probably explains her early success on the soccer fields. Molly can always make us laugh. On one occasion when fishing, she insisted on kissing each minnow goodbye before placing it on the hook.

I also remember wondering how this sisterly pair would do on their first long visit to Grandma's house. Actually, I wondered how Grandma would do. Once again, I relearned that spending time with Grandma is really all that grandchildren want. It mattered not what we did. What did count was embracing and enjoying the moment. What an adventure those four days with Caroline and Molly were! We swam, played games, went to the children's museum and the movies, made brownies, rode in the convertible. I had to buy them sunglasses, so they could be "cool dudes." I even taught them to crochet. So what do you do with a 15 foot-long red and green crocheted chain? Why, you wrap it around Grandpa's waist, and it becomes his Christmas belt.

I met Kerri and Kristi when I went to visit my daughter Laura, her new husband, and his two girls. Kerri was sparkling and impish. I could not believe that a six-year-old could be so outgoing with a stranger. She must have told me fifty times how glad she was I was there. It was easy to spend time coloring with her. We picked outrageous colors—pink elephants and purple crocodiles. When my daughter asked me if I wanted to go shopping with her, I declined. I was having too much fun with Kerri.

Kristi, at thirteen, was a different story. She was striking, with her long dark hair, in many ways already a young woman. *How would I get to know this granddaughter?* I wondered. *When would there be time to be together, one-on-one?* I got my chance the following Monday when school resumed. I volunteered to drive her to school, and since we were early, I suggested we stop at a doughnut shop. Her eyes lit up, and she really smiled at me. Over coffee, as she was much too sophisticated for chocolate milk (but not for doughnuts), she began to share about school, her friends, a particularly dumb teacher. I knew I was in when she asked to borrow my violet socks. It gave me great pleasure to leave them for her.

Emilie, granddaughter number eight and sister to Caroline and Molly, came as a surprise to all of us. Our first outing with her, when she was about nine months old, was to a hockey game. Our seats were front row and next to the players' box, a glass partition separating us. Grandpa was holding Emilie, and she was facing the box. Suddenly, we realized that these rough, tough men were cooing at her and making funny faces for her. I'm sure she flirted first.

When she was four, my family gathered to help us build a storage shed. There was a misty rain, and we were bustling trying to complete our project before a downpour came. Emilie was feeling a little left out, and ignoring the urge to direct the process, I chose to sit in my oversized, overstuffed chair with Emilie squeezed in next to me. We were all cozy, with Sheba, my cat, in my lap and Emilie's stuffed bunny in hers, and a soft blanket covering us. We talked about important things, like how raindrops make the leaves of the tree dance and how pretty wind chimes sound. She told me that she really missed Bo, my dog who had died recently. She was sad that he was gone, and so sometimes she curled up on his rug to remind her of him. She also talked about Willie, a neighbor who had died. We decided that the good thing about dying is getting to see all your family and friends who have died. "And Bo, too," she added. We played the opposite game and giggled at the ideas we came up with. She complimented me on my collection of bears and informed me that she would soon be five years old. Part of the time, we just snuggled. These are the times a grandmother treasures.

My eight granddaughters have taught me that a grandmother is not necessarily one who has time, but one who makes time. And what precious time it is.

—*Nancy Baker*

Fast Track to a Teen's Heart

Everybody remembers their first car. Mine was a 1970 Ford Maverick that my dad bought for me when I was seventeen. He paid a few hundred dollars for it, and it had to be towed home. But Dad is a genius when it comes to automobiles, and soon the car looked and ran great.

My friends and I had some good times in that car. Because it was an older model and because I was not always the most conscientious car owner, it sometimes broke down. And I had more than a few fender benders. But Dad was just a phone call away, and he always got the car running again in no time.

Eventually, I got married and had kids of my own. Before we knew it, it was time for my oldest child to get his first car. Though Steve had been saving money from his part-time job, a running vehicle was still out of his financial reach. He made us aware that most of his friends' parents had bought them cars long before, and pretty nice ones, too, not pieces of junk. We reminded him that his friends were not developing strength of character from having to do without. (Translation: If we'd had the money, we'd have bought him one, too.)

For a while Steve and I shared my car. But trying to adjust our work and school schedules around each other was getting to be too much of a strain. When my dad called to say he had bought Steve a car, my first reaction was relief. Then he told me it had to be towed home. Memories of that old, dented Maverick came flooding back, along with a new set of worries: *Would the car be safe? Would it run well enough? . . .* Of course it would. I knew Grandpa would have it looking and running great in a jiffy.

My dad had always loved cars and had been quite the hot-rodder in his day. He remembers "riding the steering wheel" when he was about four years old. The steering wheels during the 1920s and early 1930s were about twice the size they are now, and his father would sit him up there with the spoke between his legs. He rode that steering wheel like a carnival ride, dipping and rocking every time his dad made a turn. When he was about five or six, his family traveled in a 1928 Chevy Roadster to see his grandma. Dad remembers sitting in the rumble seat until a heavy rain began to pour. He pulled the cover down over him and rode along like that, as if in the trunk of a modern car, unable to see or hear anything but the roar of the engine.

By age twelve, Dad was itching to get his driver's license. He backed his dad's flatbed truck in and out of the driveway, teaching himself to drive; one day, he knocked the back porch away from the house and had to hurry up and fix it before his dad got home. In those days, you paid a quarter for your driver's license at the drugstore, and if you looked sixteen, they gave it to you. My dad was thirteen when he got his.

So began a lifelong love of cars, and an uncanny ability to keep them running, no matter what. Dad recalls driving a 1934 Studebaker in 1947, when suddenly the brakes went out. He finally got the car stopped beside the road and found out that the master cylinder was empty. Climbing down the bank to a nearby creek, Dad found an old tin can and used it to fill the cylinder with creek water so he could get home. He flushed everything out later, and the car worked fine.

Fifty-three years and a million memories ago, Mom and Dad stood beside their '49 hot rod Ford at Suntan Beach, one on top of the other. A favorite photograph shows Dad, all knobby-kneed with thick, curly hair, balancing Mom on his twenty-three-year-old shoulders. Dad fancied himself the James Dean type—drag races and daring stunts—although Mom thinks he more closely resembled young Frank Sinatra. Thanks

to my dad's tinkering and ingenuity, that old hot rod had big sun visors over the windshield, mud flaps behind the wheels, a dual exhaust system, and twice the normal amount of horse power.

To this day, Dad is still never happier than when his head is buried beneath the hood, and he immersed himself in readying his grandson's first car for the road. This presented Grandpa with a new and unique challenge, however. He had recently restored a 1967 Mustang convertible, and strangers forty years his junior had offered large sums of money for that car. So far, he had resisted the temptation to sell it, although he and Mom didn't use it much anymore. The Mustang was meant to be driven with the top down, and the wind-blown "come hither" look is not Grandma's personal favorite for attending church services on Sunday.

A classic automobile like that needs to be kept in the garage, but Grandpa's garage is too small to fit two cars and still allow room to do engine and body work on one of them. How would he fit Steve's car in there so he could work on it during the cold, winter months?

When we arrived at my folks' house to get our first look at Steve's car, we were surprised to see the Mustang convertible sitting sideways against the back wall of the small garage, with no more than an inch to spare in front and in back of it. We looked at each other in amazement. How had he gotten the car in there like that?

Well, you know what they say: You can take Grandpa out of the hot rod, but you can't take the hot rod out of Grandpa. Dad tried to tell us he drove down the driveway at a high rate of speed, slammed on the brakes just as he hit the entrance to the garage, and slid sideways, Steve McQueen–style, into the back, stopping just before he hit the back wall. I'm not sure we believe him. But how did he get the car in there like that?

So Grandpa surprised his only grandson with his first car, a shiny red Ford Taurus, which was as much fun for the elder as for the younger. It was a beautiful car, with most of the needed repairs under the hood. Steve knew something was up, he confided to me later; too many whispered phone conversations between his parents and grandparents had taken place in recent days. But the biggest joy for him, aside from the obvious thrill of car ownership, was seeing the delight in his grandfather's face at being able to present such a gift.

Steve knew he filled a special void for his grand-parents, who had lost their only son to cancer. From the time Steve could walk, Grandpa would hold him up for a peek at a car's engine or point out makes and models along the highway. Steve, belted into his infant carrier in the backseat, would crow, "Big car! Biiiiiiig car!" The posters of sports cars adorning Steve's bedroom walls were some of my dad's earliest gifts to him. It was only fitting, then, that my dad was

the one to present his grandson with the memory of a lifetime—his first automobile.

Dad had a lot of work ahead of him, and my son anxiously waited, pacing, asking to help with anything. But though Steve inherited Grandpa's easygoing nature, intelligence, and thick wavy hair, he somehow didn't get the genes for mechanical aptitude. Still, he insists everything he does know about cars came from Grandpa. He certainly shares his appreciation for automobiles.

And he knows he can always count on Grandpa. If his car breaks down or if he has a fender bender (please, God, let it be just that), Grandpa is just a phone call away and will help him get that car running again in no time—just like he did with that old Maverick of mine.

Some things never change.

—*Dianna Graveman*

A shorter version of this story was published under the title "Some Things Don't Change, Like Dad's Gift with Cars" in the St. Charles County edition of *Suburban Journal*, December 1, 2002.

Like Hummingbirds to Nectar

I used to think it was because of the junk food—the sandwiches made with a thick layer of jam spread between two slices of fluffy white bread, the petite ice cream bars eaten with the fingers, the big ripe strawberries dipped in powdered sugar.

I used to think it was because of the television programs they are allowed to watch. Or the videos they enjoy while cuddled together on the big couch in the living room—shows that, while they are not "bad," are not what my husband and I would consider beneficial and so would never let them watch.

I used to think it was because of the shopping sprees they are taken on even when it is not their birthday or a holiday or the beginning of the school year; even when they can choose something they might need for school, like a new pen or backpack, or something "special," like a trendy new outfit, cool shoes, or a toy, a game, or even a Discman.

As a young mother I couldn't understand why my kids loved to visit their grandparent's house whenever they had the opportunity. I thought it had to be because they got so spoiled at Grandma's and Grandpa's, receiving extra attention, privileges, and stuff that parents can't always give. Why else would they want to go there all the time? What was so special about being at Grandma and Grandpa's house?

Then I started questioning my parenting skills. *Am I such a bad mother that they feel like they have to get away from me? Do I give them too many chores and they feel enslaved at home? Maybe I yell at them so much that the quiet of their grandparents' house is a welcome respite from my harping. Maybe I am too demanding about their schoolwork and their behavior.*

Then I started thinking about my own grandparents, whom my children are named after. I remembered how I looked forward to my yearly visit to their homes. I would take the plane by myself and have the undivided attention of each set of grandparents for a week. I was plied with treats, taken to my favorite restaurants, entertained, and utterly spoiled. I was embarrassed when they showed me off to their friends, but I kind of enjoyed even that part.

So, that's it, I thought. *Children don't run away from their parents—they run to their grandparents.*

It's not only because they get spoiled there (which, of course, they do). It's more than that . . . something even the kids might not be able to explain. It's the whole experience of being at Grandma and Grandpa's house . . . where they are the most welcome guests. Where it is cozy, safe, and fun. Where they are always special . . . and spoiled.

Maybe it's special because of the drawers filled with knickknacks that they are allowed to empty and explore. And if they happen to find a treasure—a colorful hankie that makes a perfect doll's blanket, an old fake brooch that is in style again, or the black pointy glasses that Grandpa wore in law school—it is theirs for the taking.

Or perhaps it's because of the shelves overflowing with yellowing picture albums. They can snuggle up in a big easy chair and flip through the pages of their family's past and see what their father looked like when he lost his first tooth or how mommy looked on her first date.

It's also a meeting place for the cousins, some who live far away. They play cards, Barbies, or hide-and-seek, and forge and strengthen more family bonds. After the first contact at Grandma and Grandpa's house, they keep up the connection via phone calls and e-mail.

Of course, there are also all the stories that Grandma and Grandpa tell the grandchildren. There's the one about how Grandpa and his brother used to use their dirty socks as boxing gloves, slugging it out with one another, when their mother wasn't looking. And how Grandma hid her pregnancy from her colleagues for as long as she could, because in those days women weren't allowed to work in such a condition. Or the famous family story about how Grandpa caught an enemy soldier.

The kids also share their own stories—such as about the teacher who is unfair and always calls on Johnny and never on one very smart grandchild. Or about getting beaten up by the wild boys at school.

Then there is the excellent advice they get from their grandparents, just by asking. When trying to decide what to buy for Mom for her birthday, who better to consult than Grandma? And Grandpa always has great ideas on what to write about for those English and history papers.

Kids are also intrigued by those timeless tricks, like when Grandpa puts bread in his mouth and then makes it come out of his ear, and when Grandma counts her fingers and ends up with eleven.

Some kids even love all the hugs, kisses, cheek pinches, and cuddles that they get at their grandparents' house. Sure, some of them might run away from these or make a funny face, but that's also part of the fun.

Whatever it is that draws children to grandparents like hummingbirds to nectar, we parents should not feel jealous or threatened. It doesn't mean that we're inferior parents; it just means that our parents are superior grandparents. We should be grateful for that . . . and take comfort in the knowledge that one day it will be our turn to spoil our children's children.

—*Rakel Berenbaum*

Mama's Patootie Pie

Mallory sniffed the air, inhaling the mixed fragrance of flowers, fruit, earth, and freshly cut grass. Birds swooped from treetops and roofs, landing gently on a blossoming bush, feathered troubadours warbling a merry tune. Above the distant sound of traffic blocks away, the voices of neighbors could be heard drifting in through the open windows: Mrs. O'Sullivan calling her children; the Battaglia boys playing stickball in the street; the Sails family walking to the bus stop; the rabbi chanting, low and mournful.

Mallory peered out the window, taking in the sights, smells, and sounds of summer. Her eyes settled on a lone cherry tree standing in the middle of the room-sized front yard, a few of its aromatic blossoms still lingering from spring. The tree was the focal point of the stone-gray apartment building in which she lived with her family. Little more than a bush when they'd first moved in three years earlier, it now stretched upward in the stature of a full-fledged tree. Mallory, now seven, had watched the tree change with the seasons. At the height of summer, the bright green foliage contrasted with the deep dark red of the fruit. In fall, the leaves turned crimson, then brown, and blew away. In winter the denuded branches formed a silhouette against the snow. But the tree was at its finest in the spring when it burst forth with a profusion of blossoms. By May, the ground was blanketed with pink petals, and the first nubs of fruit began to appear.

Mallory loved the cherry tree. She could watch it from the big picture window in the living room and ignore the happenings inside her apartment, including the screams of her baby sister.

"Mallory!" Her mother yelled from across the room. "Close that window; the baby will catch a draft."

Dutifully, the girl pulled down the window and turned her back on the promising day. She wished she could go jump rope, but her mother had other plans. Dishes needed to be washed, pots and pans scrubbed, then dried and put away. There were string beans to snap, the table to set, floors to mop. Her mother ran down the list, tacking on new items as she thought of them.

The back door opened and Mama breezed in, interrupting the protest that was forming in Mallory's mind. Instead, she smiled. Mama, her grandmother, had come to rescue her from a day in the kitchen.

"Daughter, lend me Mallory. I've got to fix that tree today, and I need some help. Since you're busy with the baby, I can't ask you, and the other cousins are all doing chores. Can you spare her for a few hours?"

"I guess so. She's been nothing but useless all morning."

"I can change that. There's laundry to fold before I can get outside."

"Okay, I'll send her upstairs in a few minutes."

Mallory climbed the stairs to the third floor, bypassing her Uncle Woody's apartment. She had almost knocked, but decided not to when she heard Aunt Sally barking orders. It was not a good time to visit.

When she hit the top landing, the old floorboard creaked, announcing her entrance. Before she reached the door, her grandmother called from inside, "It's open! I'm in my bedroom."

Two wicker baskets were heaped with linen, fresh from the clothesline outside. A smaller basket held what her grandmother called "unmentionables"—panties, slips, and bras. They started on the towels first.

Mallory posed a delicate question to Mama. "What's wrong with Mommy? She's always irritable."

"How so?"

"She said I was all knobs and knees, and that I messed up my clothes, got them dirty too quickly."

"Your mother has a lot to do with the baby and such. It isn't easy taking care of a sick infant. She's just tired, is all. But you know she loves you, even when she fusses."

They folded sheets together in silence, meeting in the middle at the halfway point. Mama handed Mallory the pillowcases while she finished her lingerie. When the basket was empty, they moved to the kitchen, where Mama poured herself a cup of coffee laced with chicory. She fished in her drawer for her cigarettes and lit one up.

"We got time for a quick sit-down. How about some milk, baby? I got cookies, too."

Mallory dipped the cookies in her glass, and watched her grandmother finish another cup of strong coffee heavily doused with cream and sugar.

"Mama," Mallory asked, "what tree are you getting rid of?"

"The one in the front yard."

"The cherry tree?"

"Yes, child."

"Why, Mama? It's so pretty!" Upset, Mallory argued against the tree's demise, saying it was the best one on their block.

"Well, baby, I know. We all love that tree, but it's got to go."

"But why? Why can't it stay?"

"The city says it's sick and if we don't cut it down it will infect other trees."

"How?" asked Mallory.

"From the air, sweetie, and the bugs."

"I don't understand."

"Listen, I've got to do it. I'm the landlord. They'll fine me, and I don't want to pay the city any more money than I have to."

Mallory knotted her brow, trying to figure out a way they wouldn't have to lose the tree. But while she was thinking, her grandmother grabbed the tools and gloves, and said, "Let's go."

They climbed over the low fence and took stock. Standing under the broad limbs, it was obvious they had a big job ahead of them.

"Here's what we gotta do," Mama said. "I'll saw and you scoop. We're gonna get those cherries; no sense in letting all that fruit go to waste. Go run and get a basket from your mother."

Mallory returned with three baskets and a small pail.

"Mommy wants to know what we're going to do with all these cherries. She says we can't eat them all today."

"I have a plan, don't you worry."

As Mallory filled each bucket, she thought about how she would miss the tree. Mama said they would plant another tree, not a fruit tree, but something just as nice. Mallory couldn't imagine anything that could be that pretty.

Mama let her come up on the ladder and saw a small limb, her strong hands over Mallory's, guiding the cut. She even let Mallory taste the cherries, though Mama had warned her it would not be like the ones from the store. These were bitter and juicy with big pits in the center.

Neighbors stopped by to chat and to ask what they were doing.

"Marie, don't tell me you're chopping up that tree," said Mrs. Myers from the corner store.

Mama explained to each one what had happened and listened to the daily gossip, working while they talked. The neighbors all had the same comment: "What a shame!"

Mr. Brown lingered, hinting that Mama should give him the baskets of fruit. Mallory laughed when she shooed him away, exclaiming, "I'm not giving away the fruits of our labor!"

By early afternoon, the bulk of the work was done. Branches were scattered all over the yard as if from a storm. Mallory picked up some of the smaller ones and stacked them in a corner.

Big, fat, furry, white caterpillars fell from the sawed limbs. A slithering mass of them littered the ground near the tree trunk. Mallory tried to avoid the area, but her grandmother called her closer, directing her to hold the basket so the cherry bunches could land easily. Mallory sidestepped the caterpillars trying to get to the cherries that missed the basket, but they had quickly covered the fallen fruit. Instead, she moved underneath the stepladder while her grandmother sawed another branch. As the cherries fell from the tree, Mallory moved the basket to catch them, making sure none of the fruit dropped to the ground.

"Only two more to go," called Mama.

Mallory felt itching on her legs and arm. She thought it was sweat or cherry juice, but when she looked down, she was covered with caterpillars. She gasped, unable to move, and then cried out when one landed on her head: "Mama!"

The bugs kept falling, like raindrops. She let out an ear-piercing scream that set Mrs. Goldstein's dog barking.

"Mallory, child, what's wrong?" Mama stopped sawing and glanced down.

Seeing the problem, she scrambled down the ladder and quickly brushed away the insects. "There, there. You're okay. You about gave me a heart attack, girl!"

Mallory continued to twitch and hop around, still tingling from where the insects had been crawling on her. "They're ugly and disgusting!"

"Maybe now, but in a few short weeks, they'll be beautiful. Then you'll love them," Mama said.

Mallory gave her grandmother a confused look.

"You like butterflies, don't you? Well these creatures will turn into butterflies before the summer's end. With such lovely colors, believe you me."

"How is that possible?" Mallory put on her doubting-Thomas face, sure her grandmother was concocting a story.

"We'll talk about that later. It's time for you to go inside and get washed up. You did good today."

Mallory went straightaway to her mother, talking nonstop about her ordeal. Her mother steered her to the bathroom and helped her get clean.

"Mama says those awful things turn into butterflies. Is that right?"

"Yes, they do. Some insects go through a process that changes the way they look as they mature from youth to adulthood. It's called metamorphosis."

"Huh?" said Mallory.

"Go get the encyclopedia. I'll show you."

Unsure, Mallory brought three books: B for butterfly, C for caterpillar, and M for the other thing. Mallory's mother pointed out the pictures, the colorful two-page plate that showed the growth stages of different butterflies, while reading from the text.

"You were right," said Mallory when her grandmother came inside.

"Why, of course, sugar. Mama wouldn't lie to her baby."

While Mallory put the books back on the shelves, the women got to work. They washed the fruit, picked out the pits, and divided the assortment in half, some for pies, the rest for canning. Mallory watched as her grandmother formed pie dough like magic from water, flour, and Crisco.

"Mama makes the best ice-water crust there is," bragged her mother.

That's why the neighbors all wanted one of the bound-to-be-delicious fruit pies. When the pies were done baking, the crust a crispy brown, Mama cut her daughter, her granddaughter, and herself each a big slice of pie. The sweetened and baked cherries had lost their bitterness. Mama said the canned cherries would be even sweeter when they were ready.

"The blacker the berry, the sweeter the juice," she added with a chuckle. "Like me."

Mallory laughed, enjoying the comment as much as the dessert.

The next day, Mama was in the front yard tending to the garden. Staring at the ugly stump, Mallory lamented the loss of the cherry tree.

"After a while, you won't know it was there. Someone's coming to burn the stump, and then you and I can plant another tree," said Mama.

"Look," said Mallory, pointing to the row of tomatoes. "There's a green caterpillar about to chew on those leaves. I saw him in the book yesterday."

"Well, let's not kill him. We need to see how he's going to turn out come September."

Mallory nodded and fell silent for a few moments, deep in thought. "Mama," she finally asked, "How will I turn out?"

"Sugar, you're like a caterpillar. You may be fat or furry or green or young now, but when you grow up, you'll be as beautiful and free as a butterfly." She folded Mallory into her strong brown arms, squeezing her hard, and murmured, "You're my extra-special Patootie Pie."

Mallory hugged her back, happy to be in her embrace. Mama was wonderful. She smelled like coffee and chocolate and cigarettes and cherry pie. Mallory hoped one day she would be as beautiful and sturdy and unique as Mama and the cherry tree, growing more glorious with each season.

—Beverly A. Coleman

Legacies and Lifelines

Lizzie was the only grandmother I ever knew. I was the last of a group of four offspring, born, I suspect, long after my parents thought they were through with babies. Grandma Lizzie was white-haired and widowed by the time I was a small child old enough to remember her. But, oh, the memories!

She had become somewhat dependent on her two daughters—my mother, Della, and her only sister, Sue. She spent winters with Sue in "the city." As spring gave way to summer, she packed her large tin and pasteboard trunk and came down to spend several months with us in Lost Hills, California, a small oil company outpost in a desertlike part of the central San Joaquin Valley. Along with her trunk, she brought her beloved rocking chair, her Bible, and her cherished stash of *Unity* magazines.

I rushed to help her unpack. Inside the trunk I lifted out her corset, a mystery to me. How, with its long laces and bony stays, did that contraption ever manage to get around her body? Inside a separate bag I found lilac-scented talcum powder, a special soap inside its own dish, a container for her false teeth, denture powder, and a lovely cameo brooch. Last, I hung the dresses, mostly hand-sewn. They were made of humble fabrics, infinitely washable. Each had its own belt, sewn from the same material as the dress.

I couldn't get over my curiosity about Grandma Lizzie's bloomers. They were huge, though she was a small woman, almost as wide in girth as she was in stature. Her bloomers were always a matter not to be discussed, and she never put them in the laundry. She "rinsed them out" when none of the men were around and hung them to dry in the hot sun, so that she might retrieve them before her son-in-law and grandson got home.

Lizzie and my father had an interesting relationship. She often goaded him about how much richer Sue had married and how much more elegant was the life they enjoyed in the city. Sometimes he rose to the bait and said something rude, but most of the time he kept his sense of humor and managed to tease her in return. She, sitting in her rocker and reading her *Unity*, would pretend not to have under-stood his slightly racy joke or his innuendo. I noticed, however, that when Dad went into the kitchen to lift the porcelain coffeepot off the back of the stove, kiss my mother, and swing her around in a dance—then Grandma allowed herself to giggle. She tried to bury her face in the magazine, but I could see her sides jiggling as she struggled with her laughter.

"Oh, Della," she asked mother, "Who is that man you married?"

My brother, in his teens by then, had watched my father teasing Grandma. He decided to invent a prank of his own. He and his friend built a life-sized dummy of old clothing and stuffed with rags. They waited until Grandma brought her chair out on the front porch. There she began to shell peas as she rocked. Beside her lay a large paper fan, and she put the peas aside occasionally to cool herself in the searing desert heat. She rocked and fanned, and as she did, she watched the boys climb the ladder of an old wooden oil derrick nearby.

"What are those boys up to?" she asked.

"Nothing, Grandma," I lied.

"Well, they shouldn't be climbing so high. They could fall right off the top and kill themselves."

At that moment the boys had reached the "crow's nest." They hollered and waved just to be certain they had Lizzie's attention. Then they pitched the dummy from the top of the derrick. As it hit the ground, its head rolled free and slid down the hill.

A terrible scream erupted from Grandma. Her face turned bright red as she clasped her heart and yelled for Mom and Dad.

"Joe, Della, get out here right now. Buddy fell from the top! Someone fell from the top!"

"Grandma! It's all right!" I clutched her by the collar and shouted. "It's not really them. It's just a dummy. They were only fooling."

She sank back in her rocker and gasped to catch her breath. I could hear the boys laughing maniacally. But Grandma had the last laugh. When my parents arrived on the scene, they sent the friend home and warmed up Buddy's seat with a switch. Grandma recovered, and before summer ended it had become her favorite story. She couldn't wait to tell her friends in the city.

I expect that those friends in San Francisco, as well as my Aunt Sue and Uncle Jack, heard about how wonderful life was in Lost Hills. She probably even bragged about how well my mom had married, but only if she wanted to get a rise out of Uncle Jack.

Playing cards was Grandma's favorite pastime. Any time she found one of us idle, she enlisted us in a game of casino or rummy. She played with great gusto and she played to win.

Though we had no piano, we knew that Grandma could play one. She could sing "Swing Low, Sweet Chariot" in tones so clear and sweet it brought tears to our eyes. Her apple pies were the stuff of legends. We begged her to bake them.

She once let me trim her toenails after her bath and sprinkle her back with talcum. Fetching her false teeth became one of my chores, but I felt truly initiated into the rituals of womanhood only when she finally consented to allow me to lace up the strings of her corset.

But Grandma's greatest gift was laughter. She seemed to laugh with her entire self, giving over to helplessness. To watch her in the midst of giggling paroxysms was to lose control over one's own emotion. There were times when all of us—Momma, Daddy, Buddy, my sisters, and I—laughed helplessly in response to Grandma's hilarity.

Now I am a grandmother. And I wonder what my grandchildren will write about me, years from now—if they do. What will my legacy be? Will their memories of me be as rich as mine are of Grandma Lizzie?

Maybe they'll remember how eagerly I engaged them in games—cribbage, backgammon, and Spite and Malice. Will they think of me every time they look at a garden in bloom? How about when they see someone bury her head in a novel, or when they, too, develop a love of great books?

Above all, I hope they'll recall that I knew how to laugh. I hope they'll know for sure that I loved their parents with all my heart and, yes, depended upon them, as well. It might not happen that I will actually live with them, as Lizzie lived with us. But maybe they'll remember that we were dependent in another way—through the mutual lifeline of unconditional love.

—*Audrey Yanes*

Mud Pies

Get out of the sun," their mother shouted. "For the umpteenth time, play in the shade of the tree." The back door slammed.

The children's laughter faded, but not the buzz of the bees. The clover's nectar smelled luscious in the blistering sun. Instinctively, the bees found the sweet, no matter the location. Unrestrained, they meandered from bloom to bloom. Children play as naturally as bees make honey, and soon laughter bubbled once more from the children whose fun had been but momentarily interrupted.

These three young ones lived with their mom and dad in a cottage in the country. Their grandma and grandpa lived in the big old house on the very same property.

On that hot summer day, not far from where the grandchildren played, Grandpa puffed on his pipe while relaxing in a comfortable chair under the ancient oak tree. A wisp of smoke spiraled lazily above his head, covered by an old straw hat. He was old enough to know that without his hat, even in the shade, his bald head would suffer from the blistering sun. Once in a while a light breeze would lift the wide green leaves. He mopped his brow with a big red bandanna, thankful for the tranquility. The voice of his daughter-in-law screaming, "Get out of the sun," did not bother him. He wasn't about to venture from his shady spot.

Sounds of fun echoed around the yard and caused him to smile. The old man remembered how it felt to laugh at the silliest things and to make up childish games. Girls giggled more than the boys; he wondered why. With only three older brothers to tease him, he didn't understand girls the way he might have had he had a sister.

A mighty howl fractured his tranquility, and the painful wail assaulted his ears.

"Grandpa, help!" his grandson, Jimmy, cried.

"Lord have mercy, child. Stepped on a honey bee, did you?" He needed to stop the bellowing, or his peacefulness would vanish. "Come here. Let me remove the honey bee's tail from your foot."

Two small girls, blond hair in pigtails and not yet old enough to attend school, half carried and half dragged the bee-stung victim to Grandpa's chair.

He pulled Jimmy, still whimpering, into his lap. The child dangled while an old leathery hand held him by the ankle, and the little fellow's head almost reached the ground as both feet were inspected. Fear of the unknown choked off the boy's crying. The old man flicked out the stinger with his thumbnail, relieving some of the pain.

"Lay on the ground, little man, and put your bee-stung foot on my knee." His pipe remained in his mouth, and as he spoke, each breath exhaled a puff of smoke and laced the air with the aroma of burnt pipe tobacco.

From the small leather pouch he kept in his shirt pocket he removed a pinch of smelly tobacco leaves and made a wad by adding a little spit. He pressed it to the red spot on the hurt foot.

Jimmy looked at the wad of tobacco and then up at his Grandpa, hardly able to contain his excitement. Had Grandpa smeared a magic potion on his bee sting?

Grandpa smiled and patted the boy's head. "You'll get well before you get married."

"What?" Jimmy's eyes grew round with wonder. "Nope. I'm never getting married, Grandpa. Girls are stupid."

"I am not stupid!" Rosy-cheeked Ruthie giggled and pulled her dress up over her face, showing her round stomach.

"Instead of standing on bees, why don't you young-uns make me a fine mud pie?" Grandpa said. "I like mud pies . . . and a little peace and quiet would be much appreciated."

His daughter-in-law, Doris, no doubt wanted the same and so had shooed the kids out of the house to play under the trees. The two hickories and the oak were about the same age, but the oak provided better shade, and it dropped acorns that he raked and fed to the hogs. His children, and now his glorious grand-children, enjoyed playing under his tree. A legacy of sorts. He was a lucky man.

Grandpa chuckled. Those kids were sure to get wet and dirty making mud pies. He'd be in the dog-house by suppertime. But he hadn't asked them to get dirty—only to make him a fine mud pie.

No grass covered the ground under his tree, so there was plenty of sand in the shade, but the water from the pitcher pump was in full sun. The quest to make Grandpa a mud pie erased all memory of threats about what would become of them if they strayed out of the shade. The children scampered in the direction of the pitcher pump with an empty tin can. Their mother, who was probably sipping iced tea and sitting in front of a fan, didn't notice them bolting from their invisible playpen, for this time she didn't yell at them to get back into the shade.

His assumption was correct; all three returned to the tree sopping wet. It wasn't his fault that the pump sputtered and splashed lovely cool water. Soggy dresses and a wet shirt clung to warm bodies. Sand stuck to the wet spots, making the cotton feel like sandpaper, he imagined. Chatter gurgled and laughter still bubbled from the youngsters like the creek tumbling over the rocks, and their joy splashed over him, making him seem cooler.

With half-closed eyes, he watched a small fist throw sand into a cracked bowl and then slosh water about. They didn't have a spoon or a stick to stir, so they used their little hands to mix it all up . . . and slosh it onto themselves. When they poured the mud into the aluminum pie pan they'd confiscated from the trash barrel, as much splattered on them as landed in the dish. The older girl, Mary Beth, shook and bumped the dish to force the mud to spread over the bottom, splattering just a tad more of the gritty goo on herself and her two siblings.

The three children grinned at each other, satisfied. They'd made Grandpa's pie, and it was practically perfect!

Ruthie's chubby hands held it out for inspection. "Grandpa, here is your mud pie."

Grandpa sniffed. The crease lines around his eyes deepened. "I'm not allowed to eat chocolate. Doctor's orders. Take it away and make me a vanilla pie."

Mary Beth fisted both hands. "But, Grandpa, we don't have any vanilla."

Jimmy looked at Grandpa, disappointment pushing the pride from his face. "Can you give us a recipe for a vanilla pie?"

Mary Beth dumped the dark mud in the grass at the edge of the shade and stomped away to start again.

No matter how much white sand they used, it always turned dark when they added water.

"If we use milk, will the sand stay white?"

Ruthie shook her plaits from side to side and said, "Momma will be mad with us if we ask for milk."

"We used all the milk with our cornflakes this morning," Mary Beth added.

"I know!" Jimmy said. "We can make a regular mud pie and then pour dry sand on top." And so they did.

"Here is a fresh pie, Grandpa," said Mary Beth, "What d'ya think?"

"Yes, it's white with sugar on the top, but what's under the sugar? Give me a stick so I can scrape back the sand. . . .

"Just as I thought: It's another chocolate pie under a little white sand." He handed it back to Ruthie. "Sorry, kids, but I can't eat it."

Jimmy stomped his foot. "Oh, Grandpa, what can we do? Can we make you a grass pie?"

Grandpa confessed that he didn't care much for grass pies. And he couldn't eat chocolate, doctor's orders. It had to be vanilla, only vanilla, through and through. But try as they might, over and again, the grandchildren just couldn't make a white mud pie that quite suited Grandpa's fancy. Oooh, but they were frustrated!

Memories surfaced in Grandpa's mind. A lifetime ago he'd engaged in a similar hopeless exercise. He closed his eyes, adrift in the sights and smells and sounds of the past. . . .

The forge is hot and hissing, angered by the bellows pumping gusts of air. His father pounds a shoe on the anvil; sparks fly. The horse twitches as a fly lands on its back; nervous, it excretes droppings. What a powerful stench! Just being there—next to his dad, with his big brothers in school and no one to tease him—he fancies himself a grownup. A rush of pure exhilaration courses through his body.

"Humbug!" The old man's pipe had gone out again, waking him from his daydream. He laid the pipe on his lap, pushed the straw hat from his head and over his face, and closed his mind to everything around him, trying to kick-start his reminiscing. Ah, yes, he was back there again, in the backyard of his youth. And who was that sitting under the arbor?

Oh, yes, he could see her as clearly in his mind's eye as that morning so long ago: a bothersome aunt doing needlework in the shade arbor and demanding he come away from the horseshoeing.

> "Get away from there. You might get hurt. Do be a good boy and come here."
>
> Reluctantly, he complies. She smiles, making her eyes disappear in her dumpling face. "Show me what a big boy you've become. Make me a mud pie, and don't get dirty doing it."
>
> He didn't want to make mud pies, white or brown. But he tried. Oh, how he tried, and by his third attempt at a white mud pie . . .

A slow grin slipped over the old man's face as he remembered.

Shock forced him back to the real world as warm mud oozed down his face and neck and a sour taste rose in his throat. With his red bandanna he cleaned away the mud and glimpsed the bee-stung boy, Jimmy, shirttail flapping, tearing toward the cottage.

History had repeated itself. His aunt had never forgiven him for dumping the mud pie over her head. Would he forgive these children? . . . He chuckled. Yes, he certainly would.

—*Barbara W. Campbell*

Through the Eye of a Child

Andrew didn't care if pirates wore black eye patches like his. Besides, pirates were make-believe, and this was no fantasy. It was the real deal: an eye-patch to correct a vision problem. He was going on a much- and long-anticipated vacation with his grandma. And he didn't want to wear the dumb eye patch. I hated to disappoint him, but the doctor said he had to wear it most of the day.

His spirits improved once we climbed onto a tram heading into Dollywood theme park in Pigeon Forge, Tennessee. I couldn't wait to show him all the fun things awaiting us—the kiddie rides, the eagle show, and especially Imagination Station.

We entered the park and—after I promised we'd shop for a souvenir on our way out—passed the gift shop. The sun glinted off his golden hair as he blessed me with a cherub smile, his one eye hidden behind the patch. I felt the answering smile on my own face, the one that told him how much I loved him. I held his hand, intending to take him first to the big-rig trucks ride, every four-year-old boy's delight.

"Look, Grandma!" Andrew's face lit up with a huge smile.

He tugged me toward what looked to be a rather ordinary fountain in the middle of a brick courtyard. Andrew climbed onto the seating area and stared at the towering water spewing high into the air and cascading down into a crystal-clear pool. The cool spray misted our faces. Andrew was mesmerized by the sight; I was hoping he'd soon tire of looking at it. I tapped my foot impatiently. Time was wasting, and we hadn't seen any of the things I wanted to show him yet.

"Honey, come on. We have lots of other things to see."

He climbed down, the smile vanishing, and put his little hand in mine. Excited, I led him toward the area I knew he'd love.

We'd only moved a few yards when he tugged my arm again. "Grandma, look!"

I followed his pointing finger to a large pond. He ran ahead and pressed his face to the openings between the fence boards. The pond housed large numbers of goldfish in its murky depths, and an equal number of ducks paddled across the surface in our direction, to see if we had any food to offer. They quacked and waddled to the fence. *Ducks!* I thought. *What in the world could be so special about ducks?* I sighed loudly.

Andrew turned up his face to mine, his eye squinting in the sun's glare. "Are you tired, Grandma?"

Feeling ashamed, I shook my head and dropped a quarter in the box to get a handful of pellets for him to feed the ducks.

"Thanks, Grandma!"

He stuck his hand through the fence and opened it, letting all the pellets fall to the ground. The ducks gobbled and squabbled, and Andrew laughed in delight. Once they realized he had run out of food, they waddled back to the water and paddled away.

Patience wearing thin, I felt my foot tapping again. I glanced at my watch. There was so much to see, so much fun to be had, and so little time.

"Let's go, honey."

He reluctantly took my hand and we trudged forward. I headed for the rides, but we hadn't gone far before, once again, he tugged me in a different direction. I turned, a little impatiently, to see what had captured his attention now. This time, he'd spotted a waterfall trickling down from a wooden trough into a shallow stream lined with small rocks. He stared into the stream for a few moments and then followed the waterfall up to its source. A wooden trough carried water from a large pond at the mill to the small man-made streams throughout the park. His little face was deep in concentration as he pondered the phenomenon. I knelt beside him, hoping to distract him so we could move along.

He beamed a smile, his blue eye now on a level with mine. "It's neat, huh?"

I followed his glance. Then I saw what he saw. The sun sparkled over the trickling stream, giving light to the stones beneath. Suddenly, a childhood memory came to mind, of sitting cross-legged on the bank of a creek watching the ripples fanned by flitting fairy wings. I used to sit for hours marveling at all the mysteries hidden beneath the water's surface. Stories formed in my head that would one day find their way to paper. How different the park looked from Andrew's level.

"Yes, it's really neat, honey."

I threw out all my plans to show Andrew the wonders of the park and spent the rest of the day following his lead. We saw beautiful flowers and shrubs pruned like musical instruments. As we strolled the walkways around the park, music drifted from rocks beside the walkways. Though I knew they were speakers, Andrew showed me they were magical rocks. And, indeed, they were. At the church, we stopped to watch a chipmunk foraging for food. From a kneeling position, the park offered many wonders.

Scurrying ants aligned in rigid formation marched with bits of food on their backs. The wind stirred the leaves in the trees high above. I inhaled deeply, basking in the fragrance of mountain laurel.

Before we left we made another stop to feed the ducks. This time I stooped to gaze through the slats with Andrew. The ducks were spectacular from this vantage point. The green band around the mallard's neck glittered like rhinestones in the orange glow of the setting sun. Fat brown-feathered ducks gobbled the food pellets from my hand. Andrew and I giggled at the sensation of their beaks stroking our palms.

Until then, I hadn't realized how much I'd missed in life. I hadn't had the luxury of staying at home with my children while they were growing up. Work had always been a priority to keep food on the table and a roof over our heads. It seemed that I'd always been hurrying, trying to meet all the demands of a working mother. After my children left home, I had continued on that frantic pace. My peripheral vision was limited.

But on a lovely summer day in Tennessee I learned how to use the two eyes that God had given me. My four-year-old grandson, Andrew, taught me. And he did it with only one very weak eye.

—*Carol Ann Erhardt*

Keeper of the Magic

Easter morning! I awoke shortly after dawn to golden sunbeams streaming through the window of my grandparents' home in Oklahoma. An ardent believer in the Easter Bunny, Santa Claus, and fairies, I was too excited to stay in bed, even though I usually waited until Mama came to help me dress. I just knew that, as in years past, the Easter Bunny had come during the night to feast on the lettuce and carrots that Grandma had given me to lay beside the big bowl of hard-boiled eggs that she, Mama, and I had dyed for Easter. Then he'd hidden the eggs in Grandma's gardens, mostly in the violet and pansy beds and behind the daffodils bordering the big, old Victorian house. And he had, no doubt, also left a pretty basket filled with jelly beans, marshmallow eggs of many colors, and foil-wrapped chocolates around a large chocolate replica of himself in the center of the dining table.

My heart dancing with anticipation, I raced downstairs, stopping in the bathroom for a quick wash-up and to wriggle into my robe and slippers. I ran through the front hall and the long living room to the dining room. I saw at once that the big blue bowl that had held all the dyed eggs was empty! And next to it stood a cellophane-covered basket with the expected bounty of sugar and chocolate. I nearly squealed with delight!

Aha! I thought, spotting the dribbles of partially chewed lettuce and carrot that the Easter Bunny had left behind in his haste to finish his treat and provide mine. At last I had proof that he existed to show my friends who no longer believed in the Easter Bunny! In fact, I had gobs of proof, for he was a rather messy bunny and had left a trail of chewed lettuce and carrot that led across the floor, through the back door, and down the back steps. I grabbed the egg bowl and hurried outside, following the trail and taking care to step beside the little green and orange bits, so as to preserve the trail to show my doubting friends later.

I checked beneath violet leaves and under other spring flowers, quickly gathering the eggs and plunking them into the bowl. As I rounded a corner of the sprawling house, I thought I glimpsed a movement at the corner ahead of me and felt sure I was almost catching up to the Easter Bunny. I went as fast as I could without missing many eggs, and at last turned the final corner, where I stopped to count. Yippee! I had found all two dozen Easter eggs . . . and in record time!

When I went inside, I found Mama in the kitchen making a pot of coffee for Pop-Pop, my grandfather. Both were up very early, considering it was Easter Sunday. Pop-Pop, I noticed, was sitting at the table taking deep breaths. That was a little odd, as he usually got up first to make coffee for Mama and Grandma, but at the time I was too excited and happy for that to register.

"Mama! Pop-Pop!" I shouted. "Come look where the Easter Bunny was! Now I can prove to everyone that he is real!"

Laughing, they dutifully came to exclaim over the trail left by the Easter Bunny. They agreed that, yes, here was proof he was a real rabbit and definitely sloppy in his eating habits.

I was seven years old that Easter. I was almost twenty-seven when Mama finally told me of that morning, describing Pop-Pop's race to outwit me and preserve my belief in the Easter Bunny for at least one more year. Pop-Pop had heard me get up and guessed that I would wait no longer to start the day. While Grandma slept soundly, he'd tiptoed in to wake Mama, and they'd scurried downstairs. He'd grabbed my lettuce and carrot offerings, chewed on them, and carefully left the trail of bits for me to find. He'd been only moments out the door when I'd crept downstairs. While he had always taken great care in hiding the Easter eggs, that year he had practically tossed them at the flowers as he sped around the house with me much too close behind. He'd barely made it inside and collapsed onto a kitchen chair before I came bounding up the back steps with my bowl of colored eggs.

He and my grandmother gave me a childhood full of such memories. During the years of the Great Depression when Mama and I lived with them, my grandpa added an aura of magic that still glows in my heart. It was on his lap that I usually sat to hear the funny papers read. It was he who saw to it that my most ardent wishes to Santa Claus were fulfilled. And it was Pop-Pop who augmented the dime left by the tooth fairy if I'd lost a big molar.

Our most special time together was breakfast, when the rest of the household was still asleep. If I overslept and didn't wake up until after he'd gone to his office, Pop-Pop would leave a Lifesaver mint for me on top of the newel post at the bottom of the stairs so I would know he had thought of me.

Because of the close bond I shared with my grandfather and with my grandmother, as an adult I have eagerly waited to enjoy the other side of the experience as a grandparent myself. At last, at age seventy-three, my dream has come true. My new grandson, Michael, lives nearly 2,000 miles away, so I'll have to content myself with being a long-distance grandmother most of the time. Providing moments of magic for a child across the country won't be easy. But I will find a way.

In Pop-Pop's tradition, I will mail unexpected just-because presents and cards. I will see that Michael gets a letter from Santa postmarked the "North Pole." And perhaps one Easter I, too, will get to prove to my grandchild that the Easter Bunny is real.

—*Marcia E. Brown*

Something about Daniel

When Grandpa Towne was a young soldier at the end of World War II, his company invaded a small island near New Zealand. The conquered population was so terrified of the U.S. soldiers that several mothers, in desperation, threw their screaming babies into a ravine rather than have the soldiers get near them. Grandpa never got over that experience, and for years he couldn't bear hearing babies cry or getting too close to them. He'd look at each new grandbaby, maybe smile a little, and then go on to do something else.

Grandma and Grandpa Towne already had four grandchildren by the time Daniel was born. When little Daniel, his parents, and siblings took the long trip from Utah to Colorado to visit Grandpa and Grandma Towne, Daniel was eight months old. He already crawled and even pulled himself up on the furniture.

Daniel and his family arrived at Grandpa's house in the late afternoon. After six hours of forced inactivity, the children positively exploded from the car.

Mom put the baby on the floor in the room where the children would sleep.

"Watch Daniel," she said to his siblings and went to bring the baby's things into the house.

The older children nodded and immediately began to explore Grandma's toy box to see what new and exciting toys she had collected for them. The door from the children's room into the hallway stood wide open, with the living room right across the hallway. While the children got reacquainted with the toy box, their parents brought in the suitcases and talked with Grandma, who was trailing behind.

Grandpa, tired from a long day of work, sat in his easy chair in the living room, reading the newspaper. Suddenly, a tiny hand grasped his knee, another hand pushed the newspaper from his face, and a small body pulled himself onto Grandpa's lap. Grandpa, taken unawares, stared at Daniel. Daniel gave Grandpa his brightest brown-eyed smile and patted his cheek. Rather than touch the baby to remove him from his lap, Grandpa remained in his chair and smiled back at Daniel.

"What are you doing, little fellow?" Grandpa asked.

Daniel answered with a delighted, "Dada, dada."

"Do you mean 'Grandpa'?" Grandpa asked, his smile deepening.

Daniel, a naturally sunny child, answered with a squeal of laughter.

This single bold action sparked a lasting friendship between Grandpa Towne and Daniel. Everybody knew Grandpa loved all the grandchildren, but his relationship with Daniel was special.

Whenever he could, Grandpa spent time with Daniel, and as the years went by and Daniel grew older, he loved to visit Colorado during summer vacation to spend time with Grandpa and Grandma. Grandpa and Daniel went fishing and hunted deer. Together they worked on Grandpa's truck in the garage, talking for hours. In the evenings they sat side by side on the living room sofa, peacefully watching reruns of *Bonanza*.

When Daniel was ten, Grandpa became very sick.

Grandma called the family in Utah. "It's terminal cancer," she told her son, Daniel's father. "The doctor says he'll live only a few more weeks. He didn't send him to the hospital, because they can't do anything for him. He'd be more comfortable at home."

Even though it was the end of the summer and school would start in less than two weeks, Daniel's family immediately packed up the children and suitcases and again trekked back to Colorado. They arrived tired and downcast. Not bothering to bring his suitcase into the house, Daniel at once hurried to see Grandpa.

Like at their first meeting, Grandpa was in the living room. But the living room had changed. Now, Grandpa's easy chair was squeezed into the far corner to make room for a hospital bed. Next to the bed was a nightstand littered with small bottles of pills, a drinking bottle with a straw, tissues, and towels. The room smelled of medicine and sickness. The usually sunny living room, where Daniel had spent so many happy hours, seemed dark and serious.

Grandpa lay in the hospital bed, like a tired king. When Daniel looked at Grandpa, his heart sank. Skinny and frail, Grandpa was but a shadow of the strong, energetic man Daniel knew and loved. His cheeks were sunken; stubble covered them without hiding the sallow, wrinkly skin. Daniel sat quietly at Grandpa's bedside, uncharacteristic of his bright and wiggly personality, listening and talking to him.

Two days after they arrived, Grandpa asked for Daniel. When Daniel came to his bedside, Grandpa patted his hand. "Come closer," he said.

Daniel did, and Grandpa whispered something into his ear. Daniel smiled, nodded his head, and kissed Grandpa on the cheek. "Yes, Grandpa, I promise," he said.

Grandpa sighed and closed his eyes.

That night Grandpa died.

After the funeral, the family stayed a few more days. Eventually they had to return to Utah, so the children could start the new school year and their dad could go back to work. Mom told the children to pack their things; they would leave early the next morning.

"I'm not going," Daniel said.

"What do you mean, you're not going?" Dad demanded to know.

"I can't go home with you right now," Daniel explained. "I promised Grandpa to take care of Grandma, and she needs me now. I'm staying here."

A slow smile changed Dad's face. His eyes shone with understanding and pride. "Well, if you promised Grandpa, then I guess that's how it will be," he said.

"But he can't do that," Mom objected. "He needs to go to school. He'll miss us. Won't you, sweetie?"

Daniel's big brown eyes grew serious. "I'll miss you, Mom. But I promised Grandpa. I can go to school here. Grandma and I will take good care of each other."

So that is how it was. Daniel spent his fifth-grade school year with Grandma, and Mom and Dad visited him and Grandma as often as they could. That summer they all spent three wonderful weeks together in Colorado, and when Daniel left with his family to return to Utah, Grandma was very much at peace.

She hugged her youngest grandson and kissed his cheek. "I'm fine now, Daniel. You kept your promise to Grandpa. You go on home."

"I'll be back," Daniel promised.

Five years later, Daniel and his family moved to Colorado to be closer to Grandma, and after just a few weeks, Daniel again moved in with Grandma. He stayed with her until he moved away at the age of twenty-two, but he still calls her twice a week to make sure she's all right. Everybody knows Grandma loves all the grandchildren, but we all know her relationship with Daniel is special.

—Sonja Herbert

Malt Balls and *Dallas*

I n the middle of what seemed to be an ordinary mother-daughter chat, Dana, my twenty-eight-year-old daughter, stared me down and confessed, "I love you, Ma, and I know you love me, but Grandma gave me unconditional love, and you don't."

Was this my firstborn uttering such blasphemy? Could this heresy be directed at me? After all, during her childhood, wasn't I the one who'd spent innumerable hours reading to her? Wasn't I the one who had taken her to the beach every hot, sweaty summer, dragging along every water toy she'd ever owned? Wasn't I the one who'd played that inter-minable game Chutes and Ladders for days, weeks, months on end?

Hmmm . . . no. No. And no again. It wasn't me. I admit it: There is a long list of childhood activities for which, I, her mother, had expressed no appetite.

So, okay, it's true: I don't have much patience; I can't handle sand up my bathing suit; and I contend that Chutes and Ladders should be banned for children. Was she actually equating my inability to suffer and endure with my ability to love her unconditionally? Besides, for all those activities she always had . . . Grandma.

Maybe that was Dana's point.

Grandma—my mother, the woman who very well may have introduced rhinestones, spike heels, and jeans to the nation—was a mix of Auntie Mame and the Pied Piper. She brought out the best in people and made them feel good about themselves. Preparing Dana as her protégé, she would take her to Brighton Private Beach Club to "mingle" with the middle-aged "girls," who taught her how to "hustle at gin rummy," play championship mahjong "without a card," and maybe, just maybe, learn how to swim. As a general rule, my mother did not go into the water. Her fear was that it might dishevel her hair, something a tornado couldn't do. But whenever Dana was at the beach club, Grandma risked the fury of nature and, stoically, like a Viking, navigated Dana around the baby pool.

My mother and daughter were the only two members of a mutual admiration society. They were an inseparable dynamic duo—grandma and grand-child, whom no one could put asunder. They never tired of each other's company, and their favorite time together was Friday night sleepovers at Grandma's. Grandma would prepare crisp, well-done roast chicken; matzoh ball soup with a little rice and lots of noodles; red and green Jell-O topped with globs of Cool Whip—and, of course, anything else Dana wanted. Who knew that at the age of seven what she wanted was to watch the soap opera *Dallas* while voraciously devouring an indeterminate number of chocolate malted milk balls? Grandma, a great believer in "celebration," was happy to oblige.

It's never been clear which one of them initiated this festival, but years later, they would dissolve into hysterical giggling and point fingers while retelling the tale: "Grandma said I could," from one end, countered with "But, honey, she begged me," from the other. Although I would play along, shaking my head in mock exasperation at their soaps-watching, chocolate-malt-ball-gobbling confessions, I really didn't mind at all. My mother, always respectful of her position as deputy rather than sheriff, rarely overstepped her bounds, but when she did, it was for something worthwhile. I bowed to her instincts because I trusted them and her. My mother knew who she was.

Once, my mother came with us to Dana's dance recital. Although Dana had many talents, dancing was clearly not one of them, and it was equally clear that she was not enjoying it. At the end of the program, we approached the dancing teacher to graciously withdraw Dana from the classes. Her teacher caught us off guard. She lunged out, yanked Dana to her chest, and said, "Why doesn't she give it one more try? I think it's only fair to give it one more try." Dana's eyes were bulging and begging for rescue. My mother jockeyed for position, her flaming red hair flying as her humongous gold jewelry clanged inches away from the teacher's nose, and maneuvered Dana out of the teacher's clutches. With Dana firmly secured by the neck, she replied in her husky voice, "My granddaughter has many talents. This is not one of them. She does not need to excel at everything. She has given this one try too many." Then the queen and her princess turned on their heels and, heads held high and hands clasped together, departed the scene. Ballet was never mentioned again.

In Dana's third year of college, my mother was diagnosed with terminal lung cancer. She died ten weeks later. Dana and Grandma spoke on the phone until my mother stopped talking completely. We lost her so quickly, and I had kept Dana at bay and regretted it. They had not had the opportunity, for the last time, to kiss each other on the forehead, their customary loving exchange. My mother loved to multitask. By kissing us on the forehead, she could express her love and check for fever at the same time.

"Mommala," she would say to Dana, "I need a kiss." "Grandma, I'm not sick," Dana would reply.

"No, no," Grandma would smile. "This one is just for love."

Following the loss of her grandmother to such a swift and vicious adversary, Dana was on fire. My daughter has been compassionate and determined from the day she was born, and I love and admire that about her, but this time she was exceptionally so. She changed her major and switched to medicine in order to help "get this damned disease." Her objective, in honor of her grandmother, was to become an oncologist and do medical research. She has met her goal, after much hard work and sacrifice, and is now a physician in one of the country's best cancer centers. I know that my mother knows; I can feel it.

I am now the grandmother of Dana's newborn twin boys. I've introduced myself to them as their "unconditional love." And they seem to like me. Serving them in the way my mother served Dana will make for a challenging journey. But I am well-prepared; I had an excellent teacher. On Friday nights, once they're ready for big people food, we're going to huddle on the couch, Lucas on one side of me and Benjamin on the other, watching a DVD of *Dallas* and munching on chocolate malted milk balls.

—*Linda Holland Rathkopf*

Gamma and the Car Seat

Sasha has baby gym class at ten o'clock," says my daughter-in-law, Iulia, as she prepares to leave for work. She hands me a map. "It's a ten-minute trip."

The route doesn't seem difficult, but to be safe, I start getting us ready at 9:00. As a beginner grandmother, I'm still unaccustomed to packing a sixteen-month-old for excursions: diapers, changing pad, wipes, small toys and books, change of clothes, extra jacket, Kleenex, sippy cup of bottled water, whole-wheat crackers. After collecting these goods, I dress Sasha, wrap a fleece scarf around his neck, pop on a woolly hat, zip up a thick jacket. After a final check of the house, I pick up Sasha and my purse, sling the diaper bag over my shoulder, grab the keys, and we're out the door with half an hour for the drive, plenty of time for a wrong turn or two.

I unlock the car, drop the bags, and lift Sasha into this, his third car seat. After he outgrew the familiar infant car seat, I mastered the tricks of the second one. But this one, bought for sitters and visiting grandparents, was installed in the car by my husband, and I've never actually examined it. However, three days into babysitting, I've become a bit smug about managing baby paraphernalia. What's one more car seat?

I know to fasten the shoulder harness first, but I'm confused by a plastic bar meant to connect the two straps. After experimenting one way and another, I join the two. Now I need to fit together two oddly shaped parts of a buckle, which supposedly slips into a stationary clasp between Sasha's legs. However, for someone who once scored a courtesy five percent on a spatial awareness intelligence test, it isn't at all clear how these pieces, with projecting tabs like an advanced jigsaw puzzle, can be joined. I can't tell which way is right side up; I reverse one, then the other. They do not fit. I struggle, sweating, until Sasha complains. He likes to go, and we aren't going. I hand him crackers, retrieve the cell phone, and call Iulia.

After a stifled laugh, she says, "Suzy, it's difficult, I know, but it does work. There's an instruction booklet on my desk. Maybe that will help. Anyway, the class is not that important. If he doesn't go, it's okay."

"All right, hon, thanks," I say and hang up, still determined to get us there.

I can't leave Sasha alone and unbuckled in the car, so I unhook the shoulder harness and remove him. He begins to wail. This is not his idea of an outing. I give him another handful of crackers and carry him into the house. Rummaging through papers on Iulia's desk, I find the instructions. Picking up Sasha, I return to the car, get him back in the seat, and repeat the first connection. He wiggles and squirms.

"I'm sorry, Sasha, but Gamma's really stupid about this seat."

He nods "yes." Hoping that was a coincidence, I tear through the leaflet looking for English instructions. Lay the right part of the buckle over the left part of the buckle. Oh, they aren't supposed to fit; they're supposed to just rest, one atop the other. I try it; they slip into the clasp with a satisfying click. I give Sasha a drink of water, and we're off.

As I drive and Sasha munches, I remember how much more simple car travel was when our sons were little. At first, a slanted, plastic infant seat, thinly padded, served as car seat, play seat, and bath seat. Moving cross-country when our first son, Brad, was a year old, we turned the back seat of our Plymouth Valiant into a padded play-yard. A harness secured him to the back seat, but it tangled and he hated it, so for most of the trip he and our Scotch terrier just rolled around back there together.

Our first real car seat, a bucket-shaped plastic contraption with holes for legs and a little steering wheel, simply hooked over the front seat. Once, leaving Brad alone in the car while I dragged a week's worth of diapers and family laundry into a Laundromat, I came back out to find the car rolling down the parking lot. Heart pounding, I sprinted for the car, threw open the door, jumped in, and slammed on the brake, halting us. "Me drive," proudly proclaimed my beaming toddler, who had, indeed, leaned over and jerked the car out of gear. So I moved him (and later his brothers, at age two or so) to booster seats placed by a back-seat window. And when they outgrew those, they simply bounced around the car like Ping-Pong balls or popcorn. . . .

Then came the day it was my turn to drive in the pre-school carpool, and I was taking our dog to the vet with Wes (Sasha's father) in the front seat and three other little boys in the back seat. As we stopped for a red light, Wes, who was kneeling on the seat, must have leaned too hard on the door handle, because, to my horror, the heavy passenger door slowly swung open. Wes, clinging to the handle, drew up his legs and swung outside with the door. Seeing freedom, the dog jumped out into traffic. As the door slowly swung back toward the car, Wes, in a tight little ball, stuck to it until he landed safely back inside, quiet and pale. I slammed the gearshift into park, reached across and pulled the door firmly shut, and leaped out my door after the dog, who had run behind the car and then stopped, frozen. I scooped her up, threw her into the car, and, sweating, rejoined the commuter traffic.

After a few moments of silence, a fear-constricted voice whispered beside me, "Mommy, that made my stomach hurt."

"Honey," I said in full agreement, "it made my stomach hurt, too."

So this morning I'm grateful for safer, if more complicated, car seats. Pulling into the baby gym parking lot, I turn to the back seat. "Sasha, sweetie, we're here. And we're only ten minutes late."

There's no response. Sasha, half-eaten crackers clutched in both fists, is sound asleep.

—SuzAnne C. Cole

Little House of Treasures

My family and I edged through the breezeway of my grandparents' home, stepping between tables laden with bargains Grandpa had dragged home from flea markets and garage sales. The hobby had really taken off since he'd retired, and his treasures now filled every surface, wall, nook, and cranny of their home.

A musty, museumlike scent engulfed us as we made our way to the side door leading into the house. We passed by shelves crammed with everything from toys to small appliances from Tupperware to Depression ware. An old-time radio sat near the entrance. Dusty flues outnumbered kerosene lamps about three to one. I saw a few clock cases, but I knew the mass of working clocks lined walls inside the house—where a cacophony of ticks and tocks and dings and dongs awaited us. I opened the inner door with its familiar squawk of welcome.

"Well, look who's here," Grandpa hollered from his brown recliner. Despite its dark furniture and sparse lighting, the house suddenly felt warm and bright. "You have a hug for an ugly old man?"

"You're not ugly," I said and fell into his wide-spread arms.

"You wouldn't fib to your grandpa, would you?"

"Not unless I could get away with it." I felt his rolling laughter around me.

"You hear that?" he held me on one knee and repeated my comment with pride. He wore a crisp dress shirt over his barrel of a belly. There was a pen in his pocket and a story on his lips, the tools he had used as a salesman.

I stepped aside to give my brother a turn.

Grandpa gave him a hug and then grabbed at his nose. "Looky there," he said. His thumb stuck out between the fingers of his bear-sized fist. "Got your nose."

Grandpa sipped black coffee. I sat down between Grandma's houseplants and Grandpa's antiques, or pieces of junk, depending on where you looked. Grandpa had tried to educate us about Ming China and cloisonné vases, but there were also perfume bottles and plastic statues in the mix. The adults exchanged greetings, and Mom complimented Grandma's new hairdo.

"Oh, motor-mouth was over here again," Grandpa said. He claimed that the neighbor lady, who did up Grandma's hair, had an industrial-strength jaw that apparently was self-lubricating, because it never slowed down for an instant. "Chrysler ought to study her."

"Your Chrysler's still running?" Dad asked.

They talked about mileage and the slant six. Grandpa was a Chrysler man and told automotive stories to bolster his allegiance.

I wandered off to the small bedroom. I walked around boxes of books and then moved a stack of Grandma's crocheted afghans from the piano bench. That was where I played the electric organ that Grandma sometimes played. The sheet music was for songs like the ones Grandma had played on the piano at the country school where she taught when she'd met Grandpa.

Many times I had heard how Grandpa had an eye for the pretty schoolmistress; although he was sure she wouldn't pay any attention to a country boy who never went beyond the eighth grade. Then one day he caught up to her on the road after school and asked whether she wanted a ride home. She looked at the man wearing overalls walking beside her and laughed at his absurd proposition. He's held her attention ever since.

Grandma entered the bedroom to tell me that my aunt and cousins had come to visit. I turned off the organ and joined everyone for lemonade. The air conditioner vibrated in the living room window; I strained to hear the conversation.

Grandpa had the floor again, or maybe had held it since I'd left the room. He was glad to hear that my brother and I were taking swim lessons, but someone else was not. My younger brother feared getting water on his head; he even screamed like a tortured piglet when my parents collaborated to wash his hair.

"You know how I learned to swim, don't ya?" Grandpa started in on one I'd heard before. "Calvin and Ted taught me." He spoke of his two older brothers and how they threw him into a Kansas lake from the end of a dock. "'Sink or swim,' they said. I decided to swim."

He never did have lessons but must have learned pretty well. Grandpa worked as a lifeguard when he got old enough.

"Could've killed me," he said. "Neither one was about to jump in after me."

"You got back at 'em a couple times over the years," my dad said.

"S'pose I did." The hiss of laughter followed.

"The last time Ted stayed here—" Grandma snickered with her hand over her mouth.

"Claims there won't be another time," Grandpa began. "All because of that little clock over there." He pointed at the brass monolith at the far end of the couch; we called it the "gong clock." At the top of the hour, the chime made an indescribable hullabaloo. It was like the sound of a steam engine crashing into a trestle bridge—every hour on the hour.

Grandma served fresh coffee while Grandpa told the story.

Ted and his wife had stayed the night. Ted complained about the ticking sounds before he even crawled under the covers. When the big brass clock gonged out the hour at eleven o'clock, Grandpa said, "That old boy was fit to be tied." Grandpa looked pleased to make the announcement. "Should've heard him yelling."

Grandma obviously remembered every bit of it and started laughing with infectious hoots. She stopped to steady the cup of coffee she was carrying to my aunt while Grandpa plowed ahead.

"I thought Ted was arguing with someone who'd broken in."

"Well," my mom said, "he probably thought he was under attack."

"There was some foul language," Grandpa said. "Then it got to the point where I couldn't tell what language he was speaking."

That was it for Grandma. She started to whinny, which was funnier than the story. When the rest of us joined her, Grandma hunched over and cried as if the cup of coffee were burning her hand.

"Give me that," Grandpa said. "You're getting downright dangerous."

Grandma fell onto the couch and couldn't stop the tears of laughter until Grandpa finished the story. I became acutely aware of the unsynchronized chorus of clicking and chiming around me. I'd spent the night there myself, and it was no small feat to get to sleep. Whatever you did, you had to be in a deep, deep sleep by midnight.

My parents talked about how late it was getting, which meant it would be a good thirty minutes before we could pull away from Grandpa's conversation to drive down the street. He pointed at me. "I better get me another one of those hugs." He encircled me with his arms. "I hear you're doing good in school."

"Not bad."

"That's the way. Keep up the good work."

My brother and I tugged on Grandpa's arms to help him out of the chair. We squeezed through the cluttered rooms trying not to bump anything off its pedestal.

"See that one." Grandpa showed us a mantel clock that, to me, looked similar to ten others in the room. "Couldn't move the arms when I got it. Filthy. A woman sold it to me in a box of parts for five dollars." He waited to be coaxed before telling us that it was now worth $250.

I learned to spot a bargain myself from such visits. I didn't know how to distinguish Waterford crystal from dime store imitations, but I could recognize priceless items. The hugs, the stories, and the laughter were the real treasures in my grandparents' home.

—*Laura L. Cooper*

Just Call Me Grandma

Ray had six grandchildren when I married him, and I loved them all. Just as long as they called me "Samantha." Or even "Sam." Never Grandma, thank you very much. I didn't fit the "grandma" image, and besides, they had two "real" grandmothers. I would gladly go to birthday parties, basketball and baseball games, and school concerts. I would gladly host big family barbecues and holiday dinners. Just remember, my name is Samantha.

Then one day we went to Ryan's soccer game.

Ryan is not quite four years old. He looks so damn cute out there in the field in his older brother's soccer shirt hanging to his knees. His soccer shorts reach to mid-calf, and his soccer socks extend far up under everything. The other players are attired in similar uniforms. Although the team is made up of both boys and girls, all appear to be wearing dresses.

So there I am, seated in a folding canvas chair along the sidelines between Ray and Ryan's mother, Tracy, on a pleasant October day. I can spot Ryan by his number. I don't know how he'll find me, but somehow he looks up from the field, spots me, and blows me a kiss. Blows me a kiss! *Did you see that? Ryan blew me a kiss.*

Then he's running after the ball. What a fast little guy. He's right behind it. Has it in the perfect position. *Kick it, Ryan, kick it.*

Whoops, no, watch out. The ball's square between your feet, kiddo. And he's down. Flat on his face. *Oooh.*

Ryan lies there a while. *Is he hurt?* I rise to my feet. *My gr— … Ryan is hurt.* But no, he turns over on his side, props his head on one elbow, and watches the game for a while.

Get up, Ryan, up. Leave the watching to us. That's it. Run for the ball. Good job. You've got it. No tripping this time. Kick it. Right on! Kick it again!

He moves the ball down the field. *Wait a minute. Why did he change directions? The other way, Ryan, the other way.*

You hear all that cheering, Ryan? The other team is going to love you. You just made a goal for them!

I'm laughing so hard I'm crying. So is his mother, Tracy. Ray is still taking the whole thing pretty seriously.

"He'll learn the game as he gets older," he says solemnly. "The practice is good for them. They learn to be part of a team."

Whatever.

Ryan is running the right way this time. *Ry, there goes the ball, right past you. You can get it. Run. Run. Why are you stopping? Reaching up under your shirt? Something bothering you in your shorts? Do you maybe need to go to the bathroom?*

"Guys do that," Ray explains.

Ryan is running again. He's got it. He's fast, ahead of everyone, making little kicks. He's clear down the field now, between the plastic goalposts. *Hooray, Ryan! He made a goal! My grand— … Ryan made a goal!*

Did you ever see a little kid with so much talent?

But wait. He's following the ball right into the net. *What is he doing?* Two other friends join him between the plastic goalposts, and the three of them wrap themselves in the loose netting. They sit there a while, messing with all that cool plastic stuff.

"That's your grandson," Tracy says with a smile.

For a minute I move my eyes from the trio between the goalposts and cast them inward. *I almost said that word myself just now, didn't I? Well, I was just excited.*

A coach acting as referee trots up to Ryan and his friends, and soon they are chasing the ball down the field. Ryan closes in on it. He's got it in position for a solid kick. He aims, swings his foot, misses.

Down he goes. He pops right back up, but he's holding his arm. *Oh, no.* He's just standing there, his shoulders hunched in pain. A minute passes. He's still holding his arm. Tracy and I hurry onto the field. My breath is caught in my throat. Ryan fell hard. His arm could even be broken. But wait. Ryan is trotting down the field now, both arms swinging easily at his sides.

"I'm not going to tell you how long it takes my arm to quit hurting when I fall," I say to Tracy as we sit back down in our folding chairs and my fifty-something years settle around my shoulders. Those little kids are amazing the way they fall, get up, fall, get up, like Mexican jumping beans. If I'd fallen, I would have pulled twenty muscles, at the very least, and had to limp off the field. *Thank God, my grandson is all right.*

Yep, I said it. My grandson. That makes me Grandma.

—*Samantha Ducloux Waltz*

The Memory Shirt

Every June for several summers running, I have spent two weeks with my daughter and her family. They live in a small, quiet town in Ohio, in a big, old house that they have been remodeling since they purchased it. And every visit, I join my daughter and her five children in repairing, plastering, scraping, and painting that five-bedroom fixer-upper house they call home.

On the first morning of my visit this summer, I put on my work clothes and headed out to start working on the house. I met my daughter coming down the hall carrying a laundry basket of folded bath towels. She stopped dead in her tracks and gave me an exasperated look.

"Mom, that is so disgusting," she said.

Anything my daughter doesn't approve of is "so disgusting."

"What's so disgusting?" I asked.

"Your work shirt," she said, pulling on the sleeve. "It's filthy."

"It's not filthy; I just washed it," I said. "It's a little stained, is all."

"A little stained? It's trashed, Mom," she said.

"It's a work shirt," I argued.

"Well, maybe it's time you got rid of that rag and went back to the Goodwill store and spent a whole dollar on a new one," she said sarcastically. "Hey, there might even be a sale and you can get one for fifty cents this time."

"You're being a smarty mouth now," I said. "Besides, I don't want to get rid of this shirt. It's full of my grandchildren's memories."

My daughter let out a sigh. "What do you mean, that dirty old work shirt is full of your grandchildren's memories?"

I looked down at the stains covering my entire shirt, trying to decide which memory to start with. I decided to start with the memory of my oldest grandchild and work my way down to my youngest.

I pointed to a swath of dark red paint across the front pockets. "This is my memory of R.J. when we were remodeling the upstairs hall. Remember how he struggled to put up the scaffolding? Painting that stairway was hard work. R.J. was fourteen, and he climbed all over that scaffolding. I kept telling him to be careful, how he was making me nervous. He said, 'You always said I was a monkey, Grandma; now I'm proving it.'" I had to stop for a few seconds and blink back tears before I could go on. "R.J. will be out of high school next year and headed for the military. I won't be there to remind him to be careful."

I sniffled a bit and then looked for the second stain on my work shirt. "See this brown spot? This is Michael's memory. He was only twelve when he sanded the whole front door down to bare wood and then stained it. He did most of it himself; I helped very little. He was so proud of that front door; he just beamed when it was finally finished. Remember how he smiled when that door was hung back up? . . . With his summer job, Michael's rarely home anymore and I don't get to see him as much. He'll be leaving the nest soon, right behind R.J."

I twisted my shirt a bit to find the next stain. "See this black paint? That's Tyler's memory. He was only seven when I painted his bedroom ceiling all in black. He wanted a certain constellation of stars across the ceiling. I never could understand how a small bedroom could get so large so quickly. Tyler and I spent hours sticking all those glow-in-the-dark stars up in just the right pattern to form that constellation. Apparently it was worth all the effort; Tyler is still studying the stars."

Beth's memory was easy to find: a pizza stain in the middle of all the others. Looking at it, I couldn't help but smile . . . and think how quickly time passes.

"This is from when Beth and I got up one morning before anyone else. She was five at the time. I had gotten up early to get the back deck stained before it got too hot. She came out on the deck with bare feet, uncombed hair, and still in her pajamas, asking if she could help. With a broom handle and a paint roller, Beth stained away, getting more on her than on the deck. As a reward for being such a big help, I surprised her with a pizza picnic lunch at the park—just the two of us. That special time together is one I'll never forget."

The last memory was the newest and brightest one: speckles of white paint spattered all over the front of the old work shirt. It belonged to Tori, the baby of the family, who was growing up much too fast for my liking. She left babyhood long before I was ready for her to.

"This is Tori's memory, even though she has no memory of that day. You were out to here with her." I held my hands way out in front of my stomach. "All six of us—the other four kids, you, and I—painted the picket fence out front. It took us all morning."

Tears filled my eyes. "I can't get rid of this old work shirt. It holds too many of my grandchildren's memories."

"I didn't mean to upset you," my daughter said softly. "I know how sentimental you are and how attached you get to things like that. I should have realized the shirt was special to you."

By then I was out-and-out bawling and sniffling away. I wiped my nose on the sleeve of the old work shirt.

"Oh, Mom, that is so disgusting!"

I still have that old work shirt, and I'm still filling it with more of my grandchildren's memories. As for my daughter, she still gives me a look of disgust whenever she sees me wearing it, but she never questions why I hang on to and why I cherish my grandchildren's memory shirt.

—Mary Lou Cook

For Immediate Delivery

My daughter, Melissa, always had a penchant for, ah, a bit of exaggeration in terms of all things health. Even as a toddler she would sit for hours and affix Band-Aids all over her little person. As an adolescent, those Band-Aids grew up to be splints and casts and brown elastic bandages. That is not to say there wasn't some injury on whatever part of her body sported the latest and greatest in injury-wear. Melissa always took the position that if it hurt, it must need bandaging. Scabs were monitored with much affection, as they might require a Band-Aid should they be disturbed from their job of protecting a healing wound, a wound that until only recently had been adorned by a beloved bandage.

So it was with any viral infections and other temporary attacks on pristine wellness.

Melissa's preoccupation with disease and bandages bordered more on quirkiness than on an outright obsession.

"You know how I am, Mom," she would say after phoning me up due to a present concern that she may have contracted Legionnaire's disease. By this time Melissa was in her mid-twenties and married, and in excellent health—which she would assert was because of her due diligence in avoiding exotic diseases. If the headlines blared that a new virus was on the loose, or a bird-borne bacteria floating about, or some infection caused by monkeys, Melissa was on the job, studying and researching and worrying.

Then she got pregnant.

I must say that my daughter handled pregnancy quite well. Of course, those childbearing hips and being the perfect age for fecundity had at least some part in that. She did keep the obstetrician on her toes, though, phoning often with questions about broccoli and such. (Someone had told Melissa pregnant women shouldn't eat broccoli, and this concern took up a full two months of her pregnancy.)

At the proper time, Melissa's obstetrician suggested that birth be induced. Whatever the reason, the scheduled inducement pleased me, as I had to drive over 150 miles to attend the birth. The convenience of knowing the exact day and approximate time of birth was quite welcome.

Melissa entered the hospital at 7:00 A.M. on the day of the scheduled birth. I arrived at around 10:00, and, as I was warned, the labor was just beginning. I scanned the birthing room and was impressed by the wide array of machines with their blips and lines and one or two Pong games.

"That jagged line monitors the severity of the contractions," Melissa explained expertly, pointing to a green-glowing monitor in the corner. "The other two lines are my heartbeat and the baby's heart-beat."

I regarded this technological display of an actual birth with muted amazement. And to think my daughter understood every beep, blip, and burp.

Melissa handled the contractions admirably, though if the jagged line was any indication, the pain was along the line of a fleeting spasm caused by excess gas in the intestine. Still, Melissa would arch her back with a bit of drama that caused her husband to rush to her side in concern. The jagged line would "spike" at a level three on the monitor and then settle down to a level two. I wondered if Melissa would even know to arch her back without those monitors for cues. I also knew that when the jagged line got up to ten she wouldn't be coyly arching her back; more likely, she would be cursing the gods, her husband, and all medical personnel within earshot.

Sure, it was an uncharitable thought. So I kept it to myself.

No one was more surprised than I when the attending obstetrician announced, during a routine check for dilation, that Melissa was now at a dilation level of nine centimeters. The room had to be prepped immediately for birth. Melissa's obstetrician was called and told to come in post haste.

"Has she always been this great at handling pain?" the "other" grandmother in attendance, Melissa's mother-in-law, asked.

The nurses started bustling all about the room, wheeling in various machines and taking others out. All of them were singing Melissa's praises, this amazing young woman who was about to give birth with only a small arch of her back in response to the pain.

"She's an incredible mother-to-be," one sweet nurse told me with a smile as she pushed the small hospital crib past me. "When I had my babies, I screamed and yelled so much you would have thought I was being exorcised. And just a few minutes ago, Melissa was singing Christmas songs!"

I too had given birth, and I recalled, with shame, my demand to the physician that, the baby's health be damned, that he give me more pain medication. Yet there was my beloved, if somewhat hypochondriac, daughter, about to give birth while leading a robust chorus of holiday songs.

"I told every nurse in the delivery room that I would wipe the parking lot with them just as soon as this baby was born," Melissa's mother-in-law whispered in my ear. "Melissa is really amazing," she ended, a smile of pride tugging at her mouth.

I should have been proud, too, but at that time, suspicion was very much on my mind.

"How can she be dilated nine centimeters when that machine is showing spikes at only a level three?" I asked Melissa's mother-in-law.

Though there were numerous medical personnel milling around, I was a bit too intimidated to ask the obvious. Back in my baby-bearing years, there were no machines and cushy birthing rooms. The main indicator of impending birth was the screams and curses of the mother-to-be. Unless under a very heavy pain medication, which Melissa was not, females about to give birth did not sing Christmas carols.

The flurry of medical activity had abated. Melissa was moved to a delivery bed footed by another device that would aid in the birth. Melissa's mother-in-law dared to question the congruency of the alleged dilation with the data on the monitors.

"Dr. Rove is an excellent doctor," the OB nurse explained patiently to the two grandmothers-to-be.

"It does happen that the machines do not register large spikes though the mother-to-be is almost fully dilated. It's unusual, but the final benchmark is a physical examination, which Dr. Rove just did. He says Melissa is nine centimeters dilated, and so she is. Melissa's obstetrician has been notified and is speeding her way in."

We two grandmothers looked at each other skeptically. Melissa, meanwhile, was positioned in the birthing stirrups and graciously accepting her husband's praise with a beam of pride. I recalled telling my husband right before Melissa's birth that he should be gelded as befitting the mangy son of a (insert bad word here) that he was. Still, strange things do happen. So I figured that perhaps the Melissa of my hypochondriac memories had matured into a fine example for all of womanhood, who had, until that day, given birth amid shouts, curses, and threats that would have made the Tasmanian Devil proud.

Melissa's obstetrician hurried into the room, smartly snapping on her latex gloves, ready to do business.

"Surely she's not about to give birth?" the doctor asked an OB nurse. This question was based on the physician's observation of a woman drawn and stirruped on the delivery table as she still sang

Christmas carols and planned baby gifts with her beloved husband.

After a quick examination, Melissa's doctor snapped her gloves off just as smartly. Her face was grim and stern.

"She's not even three centimeters dilated," the obstetrician pronounced, and then sent a nurse's aid down to remove her car from the emergency room entrance.

Obviously, the vaunted Dr. Rove had made a mistake, as all humans do from time to time. It was almost a full five hours later that Melissa gave birth to my perfect granddaughter. During the birth, the air was filled with expletives, curses, demands for weapons of mass destruction, and rage against all men, who should be summarily wiped from the face of the earth. At one point my son-in-law wept and threatened to jump out the birthing room's window due to his precious wife's wrath.

No one was prouder of my daughter than I was. She gave birth in the long and proud tradition of females since Eve.

By the way, while awaiting the birth and weary of Melissa's screams, I found that by fiddling with the knobs of the jagged line machine, one could play a decent game of Space Invaders on the thing.

—*Pat Fish*

They Only Have Eyes for Pop-Pop

The screaming started at 3:00 A.M., catapulting me from a deep sleep. I fumbled with my robe and raced down the hallway to Chris's room. My eight-year-old struggled to a sitting position and moaned. Earlier, I'd elevated his leg on two large pillows to reduce post-surgical swelling. It wasn't working.

Unlike the first operation to correct a foot malformation, this surgery had started on a sour note. Another medical emergency had thrown off the doctor's surgical schedule and increased Chris's anxiety over the procedure, the pain, and another six weeks of hobbling around school on crutches. He was nervous going in. He was frantic now.

I stroked his sweaty head. His gray eyes were glazed with pain and confusion, the way a small animal looks when it's frightened or injured.

"Ooooo," he groaned. "It hurts, it hurts. Why does it hurt so bad? I need Pop-Pop."

I pulled back the sheet and touched his toes poking out from the soft cast. The color was good and the flesh wasn't warm. I ran my hand tenderly along his ankle and shin. He stiffened and yelped.

"What's going on?" my husband, John, said, groggily. He scratched his stubbly chin and slumped against the door frame.

"I don't know. This isn't like the last time. I need to call the doctor."

"He's going to lo-o-o-ve you," John said. "I don't know how Bryan can sleep through this."

Our younger son, Bryan, was the family's sleep champion. He took after me, at least the before-kids me.

"I want Pop-Pop," Chris whimpered. "I need Poppy."

I patted his shoulder and stroked his hair. "Honey, I cannot call your grandfather right now. It's the middle of the night. I'll get him first thing in the morning and then—"

"No! No! No! I need him. He'll come. I know he'll come. Pop-Pop always comes."

I looked at John. He rolled his eyes and leaned over the bed. "Christopher, be reasonable. Your mother will call the doctor and then—"

Another shriek. Chris clenched the bedsheets. His face flushed, and a thin line of sweat glistened on his upper lip. This wasn't an act. This was serious pain.

John's jaw twitched. "Call the damn doctor. Then I'll call my father."

I kissed Chris's forehead and scurried down the staircase to call Dr. Conner, who was surprisingly alert on a second ring. He suggested the post-surgical support bandage might be wrapped too tightly. The pain, he said, was a by-product of normal swelling with no place to go. He told me to stay calm. He would call the twenty-four-hour pharmacy for additional pain medication. This sounded reasonable. But for Chris, Pop-Pop was the undisputed medicine man with secret curative powers. It was a talent my father-in-law had displayed on many occasions.

Chris was my first child. As an infant, he came home from the hospital with a colicky stomach, allergies, and a negligible sleep requirement. I had little experience with infants, even less with insomnia, but I quickly learned Chris responded to constant motion—walking, swinging, racing along uneven sidewalks in a baby carriage, or unscheduled trips strapped in a car seat (a guaranteed snooze remedy).

For my low-energy days, there was Pop-Pop.

My father-in-law was still working at the time but often dropped by to see his first grandchild. The connection was immediate and strong, the sort of bond you expect between mother and child. Had I not been so frazzled and weary, I might have developed a complex or been jealous, wondering, *Why aren't my efforts enough? What am I doing wrong?* Instead, I managed to tuck my bruised ego aside and was relieved, even grateful, for the grandfatherly intervention. So was John, who was struggling with his new role as a new father.

My husband is a big man—six-foot one, broad shouldered, and husky. At the start, Chris's baby size and fragile appearance worried him. I saw the edginess in John's face and posture whenever he held Chris out like a sacred offering or touched him tentatively, as if his son's tiny frame might shatter and break.

But his father? Pop handled both our boys with surprising ease and gentleness. He'd raised two children and had years of parenting skill behind him, but there was more to it than that. John's father had a tender spot for children, something you could hear in the teasing edge of his voice and see in the genuine pleasure of his smile. In the company of children, the years slipped away and he was a born-again kid. As a doting grandfather, he was a natural.

Pop is a large man, too, with a loud voice and a sometimes heady temper. But with Chris, he was transformed into a gentle bear. I don't recall a single

instance when my father-in-law wasn't able to pro-
duce a smile, a continuous coo, or a wild peal of
laughter. Funnier still was watching them together,
Pop balanced on his haunches growling like a grizzly
or settled on the couch reciting "Itsy Bitsy Spider"
while his tiny audience, drooling and hiccupping,
stared with rapt attention.

On several occasions John had suggested we
bottle and market his father to parents the world
over. He could be the next Pet Rock, he'd said, laughingly. We could make a fortune.

After I'd thanked the surgeon for his late-night
assistance, John called his father, and then scrambled
into clothes and rushed to the pharmacy. I poked
my head into Bryan's room and smiled. Dressed in
Winnie the Pooh sleepers, he was sprawled on his
back, snoring softly. Amazing. I returned to Chris
and loosened the elastic bandage on his foot and
leg, but the pain persisted, he complained, and was
shooting from his heel to kneecap. I held him, his
narrow back against my chest, while his breaths rat-
tled in short, trembling pants. When John returned,
I administered a first dose of the medication.

Within minutes, my father-in-law arrived with a
bellowing, "Where's my boy?"

Chris's face, still flushed and sweaty, brightened
immediately. Within ten minutes, long before the
medicine had a chance to take effect, he was calm

and cheerful. And Pop? He had crawled into Chris's bed and was crooning his favorite kids' tune:

> *Round and round the cobbler's bench, / the monkey chased the weasel. / The monkey thought 'twas all in great fun. / Pop! Goes the weasel.*
>
> *I've no time to plead or to pine, / I've no time to wheedle. / Kiss me quick and then I am gone. / Pop! Goes the weasel.*

Chris shrieked with laughter. Dazed with fatigue, my husband and I watched from the doorway. John leaned over and whispered in my ear, "A fortune, I tell you . . . a magic formula at our fingertips."

The magic has continued throughout my sons' lives. They're both young adults now. My father-in-law and Chris are still good buddies, and they still make one another laugh. Now, it's Chris and Bryan who arrive at their grandfather's house for a visit and an ear-shattering "Where's Pop?" Then my father-in-law, who is not as quick as he once was, staggers up from his chair and throws his arms wide for his two towering grandsons. His voice grows strong, almost young in their company, and his face softens with undisguised delight.

My husband is now the age his father was when Chris called out in the night for the comforting presence of his Pop-Pop. Though John was reserved, even timid, when the boys were infants, he now eagerly anticipates having grandchildren of his own.

"I needed time to grow into the part," he says with a grin. "The Frey men are late bloomers, but you have to admit, we have that magic touch." He cradles his arms around a phantom baby and croons an off-key lullaby.

It's magic, all right . . . this generational gift called "love."

—Margaret A. Frey

Giant Flogging Monster

This is a story about courage, about meeting my greatest fear face-to-face. For you to understand my fear, I must take you back to my childhood.

The year was 1968. It was a very hot summer night.

We lived in a three-room house, or shack, some might say. There was a kitchen with a five-foot Formica counter, a living room with a couch and a couple of chairs, and a bedroom, which had two beds, a full-size one for Mama and Daddy and a rollaway for me. My bed was placed at the foot of the larger bed. The rooms were small; the whole house was small, compared with most. My mama was proud of her new house, though. We had moved from a one-room building with one window and no insulation. Our new house actually had real walls, windows, and two doors, one at the front and one at the back.

On hot nights, like this particular one, we slept with the windows and maybe even the doors open. None of them had screens. Being a four-year-old, I had a good imagination, and if I heard a sound or saw a shadow in the night, well, my imagination could get the better of me. My bed might as well have been in another room entirely, because I felt miles away from my parents. If I got scared and crawled in the bed with them, I would get a spanking and be put back into my bed crying.

This particular night I not only heard sounds and saw shadows, but the sounds were coming from the shadows and the shadows were actually moving. I tried to scream for Mama, but no sound came from my mouth. As I lay there too terrified to holler, the shadows started coming toward me. Yikes! I leapt into my parents' bed, not caring one bit about the consequences.

They must have been in a deep sleep, because they didn't so much as budge, not even with my whimpering and tugging at their arms. The shadow seemed to be chasing me! I tried again to scream, but the best I could do was a pitiful little squeak.

The shadow was now hovering near the foot of the bed, and I scooted as close to the headboard as I could get. I just sat there, trembling and whimpering, wishing it would go away. It came closer, as if it were walking, and then it moved across Daddy's body, and then it fell onto the floor between the bed and the wall with a loud thud.

I peeped over the edge, and just then, the shadow went to screeching and flouncing up and down the wall, and I let out a long, piercing cry. My parents instantly sat bolt upright in bed and looked at me in a wild-eyed daze. I pointed at the wall, where the shadow was still screeching and flouncing up and down the wall.

Daddy shouted, "What in the world? Get the lights!"

Mama practically fell out of the bed, stumbled across the room, and fumbled trying to find the switch. Light flooded the room, and there against the wall was a huge bird going absolutely berserk! Wings thrashed and feathers flew everywhere; the bird screeched and I screamed. Daddy tried to catch the bird, but that only made it more frantic.

Then, all of a sudden, the bird hopped onto the bed with me. And amid a cyclone of flailing wings and arms, screaming and screeching, feathers and sheets flapping wildly, Daddy snatched the huge bird and tossed him out the window.

It happened to be a huge crane that had flown in the window. From that moment on, for my entire life, I've been terrified of birds, chickens, and feathers.

Years later, I found out that there are other people who are also terrified of birds. There's even a scientific name for it: *ornithophobia*. For me, it's more a phobia of flapping feathers than it is of all birds. But it is as real and can be as debilitating as claustrophobia, arachnophobia, and all the rest of the phobias, with the same symptoms: sweating, trembling, increased heart rate, panic attacks, and delusions of the feared object being larger and more dangerous than it actually is. For my entire life, whenever a bird comes anywhere near me, that's exactly what happens.

Now that you know the story behind my lifelong fear, let me tell you my story of courage.

One warm spring afternoon, my fifteen-year-old daughter and I were relaxing in our hammocks, watching my two-year-old grandson play, while his mom and dad were out front working on their vehicle. We were just kicking back, enjoying our surroundings. Birds sang cheerfully, cows grazed in the pasture, and a mother hen scratched around for treats for her six baby chicks—which happened to attract my grandson's attention. So he started following them around and every now and then tried to snatch one up. The mother hen would ruffle out her feathers and spread her wings, and all the chicks would gather under her.

I was afraid the hen might try to defend herself and her chicks. So I told my grandson, "Stop! The mommy chicken will get you if you get too close." That made him very unhappy, and he started crying—loudly, I might add. That made the hen squawk, and that brought the rooster rushing over to defend her. I picked up my grandson, and we hurried in the other direction. I put him in his swing to quiet him and to get his mind off the chickens. Before long he was laughing and having a good time. Then he decided he wanted to play with his trucks. So I took him out of his swing, he went off to his sandbox, and I went back to the hammock to relax—keeping one eye on my grandson and the other on the rooster.

Some time passed, and everything was quiet again. My daughter and I were chatting and swinging in our hammocks, while we watched my grandson playing contentedly nearby. The chicken was back to scratching in the dirt and clucking at her chicks, and the rooster was nowhere to be seen.

My grandson waddled over on his stout little legs, almost tripping, carrying a cup of sand. Smiling proudly, he handed me the sand, and some spilled to the ground. The mother hen, obviously thinking it was feed, came hustling over followed by all six of her babies—reminding my grandson of his desire to catch a chick. In a matter of seconds, while I was trying to get out of the hammock, my grandson turned and reached for a chick, the mother hen squawked in protest, and the rooster appeared out of nowhere and began flogging my grandson.

Now, remember, I have this flapping-feather phobia, so a flogging rooster is about as bad as it can get. It's like when someone with a horrific fear of spiders sees a tarantula crawling toward them. Normally, I would have screamed bloody murder and run for shelter. This time, I could not run and hide. I had to fight that giant flogging monster off my grandson. I could scream, though, and scream I did. Shrieking like a banshee and shaking all over, I snatched up my grandson and tried to run for cover. But that little red monster reared up and came at us again, trying to get to my grandson's head, which is full of red hair. Now, face-to-face, or should I say nose-to-beak, with the rooster, I swung my arm and knocked him to the ground.

Infuriated, he came back at us. And the fight was on!

By then, my grandson and the rooster were both screeching almost as loudly as I was. Almost. I kept swinging at the rooster and trying to get away, but each time I'd turn to run, he'd come after us again and go right for my grandson's blazing red hair. Covering my grandson's head with one arm and holding him tightly in my other arm left only my legs free to defend us from the rooster. Each time I kicked him away, feathers seared my skin like fire.

Just when I felt I was about to faint, my son came to the rescue. He caught the rooster and penned him up. I was crying, my grandson was crying, my daughter was crying, and my son and daughter-in-law were trying to calm us so we could tell them what had happened. When, between sobs, we finally got out the story, my son started laughing, and then my daughter-in-law joined in. Remembering the hilarity of the commotion and her own fear of the flogging rooster got my daughter to laughing, too. The three of them kept saying they wished they'd caught the episode on video. I started laughing, too, but only out of pure relief.

My grandson survived the ordeal with a few cuts, none requiring stitches, and with no lasting phobias. He still tries to catch baby chicks. I survived the incident, too—with only minor scratches but with my phobia pretty much intact. Two years later, although I now enjoy bird-watching as a hobby, I still freak out if a large bird flies too close or if a chicken or rooster comes toward me aggressively. But if a giant flogging monster ever picks a fight with my grandson again, he's going to have to rumble with me.

—*Gaylia Roberts*

Tell Your Story in the Next Cup of Comfort!

We hope you have enjoyed *A Cup of Comfort for Grandparents* and that you will share it with all the special people in your life.

You won't want to miss our newest heartwarming volumes, *A Cup of Comfort for Parents of Children with Autism* and *A Cup of Comfort Devotional for Mothers*. Look for these new books in your favorite bookstores soon!

We're brewing up lots of other *Cup of Comfort* books, each filled to the brim with true stories that will touch your heart and soothe your soul. The inspiring tales included in these collections are written by everyday men and women, and we would love to include one of your stories in an upcoming edition of *A Cup of Comfort*.

Do you have a powerful story about an experience that dramatically changed or enhanced your life? A compelling story that can stir our emotions, make us think, and bring us hope? An inspiring story that reveals lessons of humility within a vividly told tale? Tell us your story!

Each *Cup of Comfort* contributor will receive a monetary fee, author credit, and a complimentary copy of the book. Just e-mail your submission of 1,000 to 2,000 words (one story per e-mail; no attachments, please) to:

cupofcomfort@adamsmedia.com

Or, if e-mail is unavailable to you, send it to:

A Cup of Comfort
Adams Media
57 Littlefield Street
Avon, MA 02322

You can submit as many stories as you'd like, for whichever volumes you'd like. Make sure to include your name, address, and other contact information and indicate for which volume you'd like your story to be considered. We also welcome your suggestions or stories for new *Cup of Comfort* themes.

For more information, please visit our Web site: *www.cupofcomfort.com*.

We look forward to sharing many more soothing *Cups of Comfort* with you!

Contributors

Sydney Argenta ("The Flavors of the Mix") is a freelance editor and writer. She lives in the mountains of southern Colorado with her husband. She spends her free time hiking, practicing yoga, and watching her garden grow.

Glenda Baker ("What to Name a Grandmother") is the grandmother of her daughter's two sons. She is owner and editor-in-chief of *NEWN*, a magazine devoted to helping new writers get published, and she teaches fiction writing in a local adult education program. She is a lifelong New Englander, residing in Hudson, Massachusetts.

Nancy Baker ("Pieces of Eight"), her husband, Ted, and their dog, Alex, reside in College Station, Texas. Since this story was written, Nancy has adopted two more grandchildren, Jennifer and Matthew (at last, a boy in the family). Upon the death of Nancy's best friend (read the story in *A Cup of Comfort for Friends*), she has also assumed her friend's grandmotherly role.

William M. Barnes ("Learning to Share" and "Grumpy and Poopy Doo") has published essays in the *Houston Chronicle* and in the *Cup of Comfort* series; a book of short stories, *The Nonesuch Chronicles*; and two novels, *Running Slim Buffalo Woman* and *Just One More Boom, Lord*. He writes reviews for *Southwest BookViews* and lives with his wife, Margaret, in The Woodlands, Texas.

Rakel Berenbaum ("Like Hummingbirds to Nectar") is a gerontologist working in Jerusalem, Israel, helping people with Alzheimer's. She writes and lectures about the disease and volunteers as a bereavement counselor. Although she sometimes forgets where her glasses are, she leads groups on memory improvement. Rakel knew all her grandparents and is overjoyed that her children are blessed with the same opportunity.

Mary Brockway ("A Valentine for a Neat Kid") is the mother of five, grandmother of eleven, and wife of one forever. Writing has been her passion, avocation, and comfort for more than thirty years. Her work has earned five literary awards and has been published in magazines, newspapers, and anthologies, including *A Cup of Comfort for Courage*. She makes her home in the Pacific Northwest.

Marcia E. Brown ("Keeper of the Magic"), an Austin, Texas, widow, grew up in Oklahoma and Arkansas. Since she began writing nearly fifteen years ago, she has been widely published in magazines, newspapers, and anthologies, including the *Cup of Comfort* series, and several of her essays have won awards. She specializes in humorous and upbeat family stories to preserve them for her son, daughter-in-law, and grandson.

Isabel Bearman Bucher ("Nonna's Way") lives in Albuquerque, New Mexico. After twenty years of teaching, she began her honeymoon with life—traveling the world with Bob, her husband, and resuming a writing career she thought was over when her two daughters needed college tuition. She is grateful for good health, love, friends, family, and a foundation laid by *la mia adorata nonna*, Angela Irene Giani De Bernardi.

Barbara W. Campbell ("Mud Pies") and her husband, John, spend much of their time in a cottage on an island off the coast of Australia—a writer's haven that offers tranquillity and views of the bay. Even after meals are prepared and the laundry is finished, she finds time for the computer, where she writes, explores, and corresponds with friends and colleagues.

Bobbi Carducci ("Not for a Very Long Time") lives in Round Hill, Virginia, where she is a founding member of the Round Hill Writers' Group. A journalist and freelance writer, she has published numerous magazine articles and several prize-winning short stories and writes two feature columns for a local newspaper. She has one adorable husband, four children, and four grandchildren to keep the inspiration coming.

Ginger Hamilton Caudill ("Lord, Love a Duck") is a full-time writer, wife, and mother of four, residing in Charleston, West Virginia. In her spare time, she coddles four quirky cats, a picky guinea pig, and an escape-artist hamster. Caudill's stories are featured in numerous publications, including *StorySouth*, *Mountain Echoes*, *Dead Mule*,

Front Porch, The Pen Point View, Unlikely Stories, Penwomanship, and in several anthologies.

Mahala Church ("Love-a-Bye") is a business and technical writer and editor who writes from her life experience and from her previous career as a registered nurse. Inspired by her love for Southern literature, she also writes children's books, essays, and fiction. She lives in Mobile, Alabama, with her daughter, granddaughter, two spoiled dogs, and a turtle who loves grits.

SuzAnne C. Cole ("An American Babushka" and "Gamma and the Car Seat") has one grandson and is expecting two more grandchildren soon. When not playing cars, giving voice to puppets, or inventing stories about Sasha and his naughty alter-ego, Sam, she writes. More than 300 of her essays, poems, plays, and short stories have been published in a wide variety of anthologies, newspapers, and commercial and literary magazines.

Beverly A. Coleman ("Mama's Patootie Pie"), a longtime Midwesterner and information technology professional, has written all her life. A Louisiana native, her family roots are Southern, providing inspiration for many tales. She recently moved to Virginia, where she continues to write stories about diversity while working for a high-tech consulting company.

Karna J. Converse ("Tales in a Teapot"), a freelance writer, lives in Storm Lake, Iowa, with her husband and three children. Her favorite tea is ginger peach, but she'll "take tea" with chocolate milk in Gram's teapot whenever her daughter asks.

Mary Lou Cook ("The Memory Shirt") has written short stories and devotionals for a number of years. She spends her summers in New York and her winters in Florida. Her home is a fifth-wheel RV she shares with her husband, with whom she also shares a blended family of six children and sixteen grandchildren.

Laura L. Cooper ("Little House of Treasures") is a communications specialist, homeschool teacher, and freelance writer in Nebraska. Her fiction and nonfiction stories have appeared online and in print. She is a member of the Nebraska Writers Guild and the National Association of Women Writers.

Darla Curry ("Toy Box Confidential") is an award-winning freelance writer whose nonfiction stories have appeared in Texas newspapers. She lives in The Woodlands, Texas, with her husband. She believes humor and grandkids are necessary ingredients of the recipe for a great life. She exercises and speed-walks to keep pace with her four "grands."

Cathy Elliott ("Tender Hearts") works in a community college library in beautiful northern California. She loves antiquing, quilting, and playing her guitar, but writing is her passion. Her first novel, a cozy mystery titled

A *Vase of Mistaken Identity*, published by Kregel Publishing, was released in spring 2006.

Carol Ann Erhardt ("Through the Eye of a Child") lives with her husband, Ron, and their three cats—Wilbur, Charlotte, and Templeton, named after the characters in *Charlotte's Web* (E. B. White). This mother of eight and grandmother of twenty-two is an avid reader and author who is currently working on her second novel.

Pat Fish ("For Immediate Delivery") lives in Georgetown, Delaware, where her backyard has been certified by the National Wildlife Federation as a Backyard Wildlife Habitat. She is also certified as a Backyard Wildlife Steward. This love for the critters of her eco-garden is reflected in much of Pat's writing. She pens pieces about gardens, birds, and politics, and can also churn out a cozy mystery now and then.

Margaret A. Frey ("They Only Have Eyes for Pop-Pop") writes from the foothills of the Smoky Mountains. Her fiction and nonfiction have appeared in print and online, including *Writer's Digest, Byline Magazine, Rocking Chair Reader, Christian Science Monitor, Mindprints Literary Journal, Kaleidoscope Magazine*. She lives with her husband, John, and canine literary critic, Ruffian.

Jodi Gastaldo ("The Froufrou Room") lives in a Cleveland, Ohio, suburb with her husband, Dan, daughter, Maggie, and son, Ben. She balances motherhood and womanhood with the help of many wonderful grandparents (both hers and her kids). In her rare free time, she works in operations at a bank, escapes to the movie theater, and enjoys writing stories.

Dianna Graveman ("Fast Track to a Teen's Heart") currently teaches third grade. She earned a bachelor's degree in education from the University of Missouri and an M.F.A. degree in writing from Lindenwood University. She lives in St. Charles, Missouri, with her husband, three almost-grown children, and a lovable mutt named Tramp.

Valerie Kay Gwin ("The Land of That's Okay") is a freelance writer living in Kearney, Nebraska, with her husband and their teenage son. She is employed part time as an educational administrative assistant and is an active member of the Central Nebraska Fellowship of Christian Writers, Artists, and Musicians.

Denise Heins ("She's Back and She's Brought Something with Her") is a homemaker who enjoys cooking, reading, gardening, and enjoying life in the beautiful Missouri Ozarks. She shares her days with her husband, Dave, daughter, Jennifer, and son, Josh. Her grandson James recently celebrated his fifth birthday and welcomed his baby brother, Rylee, to the family.

Sonja Herbert ("Something about Daniel") is a freelance writer and novelist. Her novel *Tightrope!* tells the story of her mother hiding in a circus during Hitler's reign.

Sonja was born in that circus. She now lives in Oregon with her husband, the last of her six children, and two cats.

Reneé Willa Hixson ("When the Going Gets Tough, Get Grandma") is a homemaker and freelance writer. She lives in Surrey, British Columbia, Canada, with her husband and four children. Much of Reneé's childhood was enriched by a grandmother living in her home, and for a short time both of her grandmothers lived with Reneé's family.

Jo Ann Holbrook ("Me, a Grandmother? No Way!") is a freelance writer, weekly columnist, and award-winning feature writer whose articles appear in numerous newspapers and magazines, including *Western Mule, Evansville Living,* and *Outdoor Sports in the Southeast.* On their 10-acre mini-farm, she and her husband, Gil, share life with two dogs, horses, chickens, and on special days, their granddaughter.

Dennis Jamison ("Grandma Will Save Me") works as a customer correspondence specialist with a medical device company based in northern California. He received a bachelor of arts from the University of Iowa. Although he grew strong roots in Iowa, he has been successfully transplanted into the San Francisco Bay area, where he currently lives with his wife and three teenagers.

Sally Kelly-Engeman ("Sounds of Love") is a freelance

writer who has had numerous short stories and articles published. A resident of Loveland, Colorado, she enjoys traveling around the world with her husband. She also enjoys reading, researching, writing, attending the theater, ballroom dancing, family gatherings, and, of course, being a grandmother.

Miriya Kilmore ("Raising Adam"), of Sylmar, California, has enjoyed a lifelong love affair with words and horses. She first sat in a saddle at six months and began reading before kindergarten. Both of these passions have proven valuable and never more so than when her grandson needed her most. To share the enormous amount of research she has collected, Ms. Kemsley started a newsletter and online discussion group for grandparents raising grandkids.

Charles Langley ("My Granddaughters, My Life") is retired and makes his home in Rochester, New York. Since returning to writing after a fifty-nine-year hiatus, he has written more than 100 short stories, poems, and articles for magazines, e-zines, and books, including *A Cup of Comfort for Inspiration*. In 2003, Gannett Newspapers ran his full-page account of being a cub reporter covering the trial of Bruno Richard Hauptmann, who was convicted in 1935 of kidnapping the baby son of Charles and Anne Lindbergh.

May Mavrogenis ("Vindication") was born in Paris, France. She married John, a Greek, and together they raised two children, Marcel and Agnes. They make their home in Clinton, New York, where he worked as an administrator at Hamilton College and she as a French teacher in the local high school. Since retiring from teaching, May has enjoyed being able to do anything she wants, including writing.

Susan Billings Mitchell ("Actually, That's My Grandpa") is a happy wife, homemaker, and mother of nine grown children. Her favorite job is being a full-time grandmother. Her hobbies are writing, storytelling, and puppetry. At present, her priority in life is to create joyful memories for each of her twenty-one grandchildren.

Camille Moffat ("When the Time Is Right") lives in the Blue Ridge Mountains, overlooking the Shenandoah Valley. She has been writing all her life and does reasonably well at it, which is a good thing, since she's not really suited to do anything else.

Art Montague ("Grandpa in Charge") is a professional freelance writer whose rambunctious though loveable granddaughter has been front and center since he returned to full-time writing in the year 2000. "Grandpa in Charge" was written during K.C.'s toddler years, when Grandpa did more than his fair share of babysitting.

Sheila Moss ("How to Spoil a Grandchild and Alienate a Daughter-in-Law in One Easy Lesson") is a grandparent as well as a humor columnist. She admits to being a mother-in-law, but was also a daughter-in-law at one time. She denies that she could possibly be guilty of giving unsolicited advice. Her articles have been widely published, and her weekly column appears in several newspapers as well as online.

Linda Holland Rathkopf ("Malt Balls and *Dallas*") is a writer and artist. Her artwork has been shown at galleries throughout the northeastern United States. Her illustrations have been seen in books and calendars. Three of her plays, "Who Stole the Mona Lisa?," "The Kindling Effect," and "The Airport Encounter," have been produced in New York City. She makes her home in Brooklyn, New York.

Gaylia Roberts ("Giant Flogging Monster") lives with her husband and daughter in a small rural town in Oklahoma. She also has a son and two grandchildren. She enjoys reading, gardening, arts and crafts, and writing about life's experiences.

Virginia Rudd ("Life Cycles") left college intending to write the great American novel. Life and reality intervened. Now, semi-retired from a long career as a copywriter, she is rekindling her dream of becoming a "real" writer. She lives in Cheshire, Connecticut, near her two daughters, three granddaughters, and the grandson who inspired "Life Cycles."

Susan J. Siersma ("Jooots and Ohk"), a former special education aide, shares her home in beautiful northern New Jersey with her husband, Rodger. She has happily raised kids, cats, dogs, chickens, gardens, butterflies, and possibly a few eyebrows. She cherishes time spent with family, especially her four grandchildren. Several of Susan's stories have been published in inspirational books, including the *Cup of Comfort* series.

Libby Simon ("How Do I Love Thee?") is a retired school social worker. Now a freelance writer, she writes humor and slice-of-life pieces as well as essays on social/educational issues. She has been published in both U.S. and Canadian newspapers, magazines, scholarly journals, and anthologies, including other volumes of *A Cup of Comfort*. Her booklet on a violence prevention program for kindergarten to grade three, *Don't Fight, It's Not Right*, is available online through the Manitoba Text Book Bureau.

Mike Tolbert ("A Grandfather's First Letter to His Grandson"), a former political reporter, has enjoyed a highly successful, thirty-year career as a public relations professional specializing in strategic marketing plans for corporations and political candidates. His passions are his wife, Annette, who recently retired after thirty-five years as a second-grade teacher, and their five horses and six grandchildren.

Samantha Ducloux Waltz ("Birth of a Family" and "Just Call Me Grandma") and her husband, Ray, live in Portland, Oregon, where their large, blended family keeps them busy and proud. A retired teacher and a freelance writer, she has published fiction and nonfiction under the names Samellyn Wood, Samantha Ducloux, and Samantha Ducloux Waltz. Her personal essays have appeared in *The Christian Science Monitor* and a number of anthologies, including *A Cup of Comfort*.

Anne C. Watkins ("The Indomitable Miss Chelsea"), a full-time freelance writer, is the author of *The Conure Handbook,* and her writing has appeared in numerous print magazines, Web sites, and anthologies. She and her banjo-player husband, Allen, live in Vinemont, Alabama, where they love to spoil their grandchildren, Chelsea, Bailey, and Tyler.

Audrey Yanes ("Legacies and Lifelines") is a retired kindergarten teacher and the mother of nine children. She has stood on the Great Wall in China, studied in the Galápagos, sailed the islands of Greece, and prayed at the Wailing Wall in Jerusalem. When not working on her memoirs, she enjoys rafting and writing poetry. Another of her stories appears in *A Cup of Comfort for Sisters*.

About the Editor

Colleen Sell is the editor of fourteen volumes in the *Cup of Comfort* anthology series. During her long career in words, she has been a book author, editor, and ghostwriter; magazine editor and features writer; journalist; tech writer; and copywriter.

She shares a big old house on a lavender farm in the Pacific Northwest with her husband, T. N. Trudeau. Her brilliant and beautiful grandchildren are among their most cherished guests.

The *Cup of Comfort* Series!

All titles are $9.95 unless otherwise noted.

A Cup of Comfort
1-58062-524-X

A Cup of Comfort Cookbook ($12.95)
1-58062-788-9

A Cup of Comfort Devotional ($12.95)
1-59337-090-3

A Cup of Comfort Devotional for Women ($12.95)
1-59337-409-7

A Cup of Comfort for Christians
1-59337-541-7

A Cup of Comfort for Christmas
1-58062-921-0

A Cup of Comfort for Friends
1-58062-622-X

A Cup of Comfort for Grandparents
1-59337-523-9

A Cup of Comfort for Inspiration
1-58062-914-8

A Cup of Comfort for Mothers and Daughters
1-58062-844-3

A Cup of Comfort for Mothers and Sons
1-59337-257-4

A Cup of Comfort for Mothers to Be
1-59337-574-3

A Cup of Comfort for Nurses
1-59337-542-5

A Cup of Comfort for Sisters
1-59337-097-0

A Cup of Comfort for Teachers
1-59337-008-3

A Cup of Comfort for Weddings
1-59337-519-0

A Cup of Comfort for Women
1-58062-748-X

A Cup of Comfort for Women in Love
1-59337-362-7